To: Alvin and Lucille Harrell

From: The Foundation for Evangelism
Nashville, Tennessee.
Charles E. Kinder, President
10-6-82

HARRY DENMAN
A Biography

HARRY DENMAN

A Biography

HAROLD ROGERS

THE UPPER ROOM

Harry Denman: A Biography

The Upper Room Disciplines is an annual publication of The Upper Room. Quotations in this book include an indication of the volume year in which the meditations appeared. ©1961 and 1967.

Library of Congress Catalog Card Number: 77-93277

UR-369-5-1177 (paperback)
UR-370-2-1177 (hardback)

for
Lou Dozier

CONTENTS

Following page 64 is an eight-page photo section on the life and career of Harry Denman.

PREFACE

Harry Denman's body died on November 8, 1976. A driving force, which had been felt all across North America and into the far reaches of the world, became then a memory. He was mourned by taxi drivers and educators, convicts and bishops, blacks and whites, orientals and American Indians as a true friend who had in some measure made life more significant to them. The man who had shunned publicity all of his life was suddenly in the headlines. Superlatives poured from pens and typewriters.

Those who conducted the brief committal service carried out his request for no eulogy. A lifelong friend writing of the occasion said, "How characteristic! Harry Denman would be the last man in the world who would desire laudatory remarks about himself at his burial. However, his whole life was a paean of praise to God."

Dr. Billy Graham telegraphed: "Just heard that the Lord has taken one of his greatest servants, Harry Denman, to heaven. I had no better friend or greater supporter or better counselor in my evangelistic work than Harry Denman. I shall greatly miss him."

A bishop described him as the kind of man who could carry the flag at the head of the parade and at the same time beat the drum setting the cadence for the march.

To meet him was to feel the force of his personality and be challenged by it. The impact of his spiritual and physical presence is not easily forgotten. He moved tirelessly, confidently, dedicated to one objective—to witness for the Lord Jesus Christ.

When he was part of a group, whether with colleagues or strangers, businessmen or politicians, invariably the conversation shifted to the Bible, prayer, and the risen Lord, whom he served. He commanded attention by his dedication and singleness of purpose. A layman, not a preacher, he had the gift of making people want to listen whether he was speaking with just one person or to a multitude.

He was a man who never accepted no as final. When told that a certain thing could not be done, he inevitably countered, "Have you tried it?" He would immediately suggest any number of methods of attack.

His was a force to be reckoned with. His extended hand was out, ready to lift the unfortunate to a higher level, yet he did not bypass the "up and out." An airline captain, a bishop, a statesman—Harry Denman was as ready with a word of encouragement and a sincere prayer for them as he was for the porter in a rest room.

Love for his Lord and for his fellow human beings

was the keynote of his life. The things he stood for were many of those that are now coming to pass but were not popular in his day; the equality of persons regardless of sex, nationality, or race; simplicity; the discarding of the false values of a materialistic world; and a search for the true values of life as taught by Jesus in the Sermon on the Mount.

When he died there was still so much that he wanted to do. The organizations which he had helped to found were growing. There were more prayers to be prayed, more letters to be written, more people to be encouraged, more churches to be started, more witnessing to be done. So much more.

To write about Harry Denman, to separate fact from legend, to search his letters, read the notations in his Bible, to hear the testimonies and anecdotes of his former colleagues and admirers, to listen to the tapes of his sermons—this has been a monumental task. I have undoubtedly left many avenues unexplored. For those who will be aware of such omissions and inaccuracies I can only borrow a phrase often used by the one about whom this book is written: "Pray for me."

HAROLD ROGERS

ACKNOWLEDGEMENTS

I AM MOST GRATEFUL to my former colleagues Lou Dozier, Harold Hermann, D. E. Jackson, Brooks Little, and Sulon Ferree, who have aided me in research, and have relived with me some of the experiences we shared together as staff members of the General Board of Evangelism while Dr. Harry Denman was general secretary.

Ruth Hill Badeau, Edwin Branscomb, John Bryan, Philip C. Jackson, and Joe Travis, residents of Birmingham, Alabama; Mrs. W. Angie Smith of Dallas, Texas; and Walter Sherman, Bismarck, North Dakota—all longtime friends of the one about whom this book is written—have been so gracious to reply to my many questions.

To all of these I wish to express my heartfelt thanks.

H.R.

HARRY DENMAN
A Biography

1

OBSCURE YEARS

Harry Denman was a very private person. Ready to share his faith with all, he would bury deep his hurts, his loneliness, his sorrows. While he walked many times with others in their griefs, too often there was no one to walk with him. He did not open the door to his inner self. He would not burden friends with his personal problems and memories. As a result, we know little of his early years.

We can catch a glimpse of the poverty he and his mother knew by a sentence in a letter, a phrase in a sermon or an article. We know he left school at the age of ten to support himself and his mother.

In a brief article he wrote, "I remember when I was a boy in Smithfield, every Saturday afternoon my responsibility was to go to St. Paul's Church with old newspaper and clean the oil lamps. I was the maintenance man. I rang the bell on Sunday and Wednesday night. The big old bell would lift me from the floor, but I always came back down."

Harry Denman's parents, William Henry and Hattie Leonard Denman, were born in Gloucestershire, England, and immigrated to Birmingham, Alabama where he was born September 26, 1893. His father worked there as a molder in one of the foundries. According to those who remember, when Harry was nine years old the father "just up and left."

Some years later Harry Denman learned that his father had gone to Pittsburgh, Pennsylvania, where he followed his trade as a foundry worker. Naturalization papers, recorded there, give the date April 22, 1911, when William Henry Denman, aged fifty-seven, became a United States citizen. It is believed that the father probably had some contact with his wife and son in Birmingham, but apparently he never returned. Additional records indicate that his father died September 11, 1927, and was buried in Pittsburgh. His mother died in 1937 in Birmingham at the age of seventy-two and was buried there.

In 1956 Harry Denman and J. Manning Potts tried to locate Dr. Denman's relatives in England, but they were unable to do so. So far as Harry Denman was able to learn, he had no living relatives either in England or the United States. He recalled having been in England with his mother when he was six years old and was able to locate the graves of his grandparents and the house where they had lived, but that was all.

Along the way there were three persons, other than his mother, who seemed to have influenced his life for the better. In a sermon he told of a pastor who made time for children. "On Sunday afternoon, when he had already preached twice, he would meet with the children at four o'clock. He taught us how to worship in church. He taught us how to pray. He taught us how to enter the sanctuary and worship through prayer and meditation. He taught about forty-five boys and girls. His name was Samuel R. Lester. He was not a college graduate, certainly he never attended seminary, but he loved children."

Then there was the Reverend L. C. Branscomb. He was holding a revival in the Smithfield Church when Harry Denman made a public declaration for Jesus Christ. Sensing something of the outstanding qualities and desires of this young man, Mr. Branscomb encouraged him to further his education.

About that time there was a Sunday School worker who had a great influence on him. Many years later in writing a tribute to her, he said, "One person influenced my life perhaps more than any other except my mother. This person led me to give my life to Christ for full-time service. She interested me in the work of religious education because she gave her body, mind, heart, and soul to the cause. This woman was Miss Minnie E. Kennedy."

With Miss Kennedy to encourage him and the Reverend L. C. Branscomb to make some funds available, Harry Denman decided to go back to school and pick up where he had left off in 1904. While quite young he had gone to work for the Tennessee Coal and Iron Company, first as an errand boy and later in other capacities. In 1915 he resigned to become the secretary of the Birmingham Sunday School Council for thirty dollars a month. He remained there until 1919 when he became business manager for the First Methodist Episcopal Church, South, in Birmingham, a position he held until 1938. At that time he was elected secretary for the Department of Evangelism in the Board of Missions of the Methodist Episcopal Church, South, in Nashville, Tennessee.

Despite his many responsibilities with the church and at home, Harry Denman entered preparatory school at the age of twenty-two, then continued at Birmingham Southern College, receiving a B.A. degree in 1921 and an M.A. degree from the same school in 1930.

In a meditation he wrote for *The Upper Room* (June 14, 1973), he gave a glimpse of his struggle to obtain an education:

> I entered first year preparatory school in Birmingham College in September 1915. I wanted an education, so I quit my job for a part-time job which paid one third of what I had been making. The slow pace of college discouraged me. I wanted to go back to the business world.
>
> One morning I stood in the Chapel looking out the window trying to decide what to do. An upperclassman came and stood by my side. "Harry, we are glad you have entered school. We are going to stay by you. You have our prayers and help." He walked away. I decided to stay.

The upperclassman was Bachman G. Hodge, who later became a bishop in The Methodist Church.

Much later, responding to someone who was experiencing health problems, he confided, "I worked very hard for six long years to get an education. I worked day and night. I did not have sufficient food. I received the education, but a year or two later my body broke. I was upset emotionally. I had a good doctor. He told me what I needed was to go to bed at night and eat certain foods. I did this for a year or two and was well, but I know what it means to be emotionally upset."

With a quick change of pace he was adroit at sidestepping questions he did not want to answer. When he was forty-five, after he had moved to Nashville, a woman wrote she was worried about his not getting married. He replied, "I think I am a little bit old and have lost my nerve. However, Gypsy Smith finally got married. Perhaps I am not old enough."

Demanding as his work was as business manager of a large metropolitan church, he still found time to organize the Older Boy's Council. This large group of older boys met in the Sunday school office downtown at seven o'clock on Sunday morning to preview the week's lesson. Then they went to share in the Sunday school classes of their respective churches.

In the church where he served as business manager, he also organized a girl's class which soon became one of the largest Sunday school classes in the Methodist Episcopal Church, South. That class is still in existence, and some of the original members are now grandmothers in their church.

Always the organizer and much interested in recreational activities for young persons, he worked for the establishment of Camp Winnataska, and made it possible for many young people to attend.

Still another glimpse of this man, who would later forget holidays, comes from his classmate and longtime friend, the Reverend Dr. Edwin Branscomb: "Some people stand in awe of a completely dedicated Christian, but as you know there are some telltale clues that mark each one as human. Harry was expelled during his college days for being a rabble-rouser and demanding a holiday from the college administration. However, after one day of cutting classes, he returned to the president's office, apologized, and was promptly reinstated."

This "rabble-rouser" was also awarded two honorary doctorates, one from Athens College, Athens, Alabama, and the other from Ewha Woman's University, Seoul, Korea. When questioned about his education in an interview with a reporter from the *Atlanta Constitution,* he quipped, "The doctor handle was a store-bought D.D., twenty-five dollars a D."

One very poignant insight comes from a sermon he preached after he had retired:

Thanksgiving, 1936, I was speaking to the North Georgia Conference. I was away from home. I always gave Saturday night to my mother, and all the holidays were given to her. Saturday night was hers. We used to play dominoes together that evening. Sometimes though I would have to leave to go to the jail to get somebody out or go to the hospital to see somebody dying or go to the undertakers.

But I was away from my mother on Thanksgiving. That had never happened before, so I wrote her a letter and told her how sorry I was. I think I was a little homesick. I told her how much I appreciated the way she did without things so I could go to school. She did without food. She did without clothes. I just wrote and thanked her. Three months later, in 1937, her body died, and she went to be with the Lord.

Harry Denman never spoke of a person as having died. Always it was the body that had died, and he always used the phrase *coronation service* rather than the word *funeral.*

For Easter, 1937, Harry Denman wrote a card which he had printed and sent to his friends who had helped strengthen him in the loss of his mother.

I will not say she is dead.
    "Because I live—ye shall live also."
In beautiful Elmwood, released from suffering,
    Her tired body rests,
Her courageous soul is with the living Christ.

From the nearby trees—spring melodies are sung
    By her Father's feathered choir.
This morning in the Heavenly Choir she sings
    "Perfect submission—all is at rest
    I in my Savior am happy and blest."

On the final Resurrection morning
    I expect to see the beautiful spirit of my mother.

2

THE ORGANIZATION MAN

HARRY DENMAN was an organization man.* While every member of his staff had an assigned area of responsibility—editorial, field, business—he demanded that they be team players. Once a program was adopted, laity and clergy worked in unison. From time to time a staff person might leave the organization, but the great majority were long termers with ten, fifteen, twenty, or more years of service.

Bishop Paul B. Kern wrote, "I am constantly amazed at the power of your organization. They impress me as men 'whom a dream hath possessed,' a dream of Christian America, of a reborn Methodism and the coming of the Kingdom."

Harry Denman knew the entire church as few other persons did. He was on intimate terms with the problems of the individual churches, but he was

---

* Author's Note: No attempt is made in this book to tell the story of the General Board of Evangelism of The Methodist Church, which Harry Denman served as general secretary from its beginning until his retirement in 1965. That story is told in complete detail in the book, *Thy Kingdom Come* written by Charles M. Laymon and published by the General Board of Evangelism in 1964.

also very much a part of the bureaucracy. While he often appeared to move in an ethereal atmosphere, his hands were always down in the grease and the grime of the machinery, and he could be its most severe critic.

To a friend he confided, "I am having a rather hard time with Christians or church members, whichever you desire to call them. They do a lot of praying, but they want God to do everything. They ask God to save sinners. They ask God to bring people to the services. I tell them that I do not see how God is going to do it. He does not run a taxicab. Jesus never said, 'Pray for sinners.' He said, 'Pray for laborers.' People do not believe that. I think most Christians are just downright lazy. We want God to do everything."

Time after time he spoke out about the church breaking up families. "We have activities for the men. We have activities for the women. We have activities for teenagers. We have activities for the young married couples, and we have activities for children. Consequently the family is never together.

"I think the church ought to say, 'This is going to be family night. But instead of spending it at the church, we are going to spend it at home. Every family is going to have a service at home.' I do not mean a long service. Perhaps the family would sing a few hymns, have a prayer, read the scripture, and talk about it. That would keep the family together in the home where they need to be."

The North Alabama Conference elected him a

delegate to the Southeastern Jurisdictional Conference in 1940, 1944, and 1952, and to the General
Conference in 1934 and 1938, the Uniting Conference in 1939, and the General Conference in 1940
and 1952.

He left his position in the local church in 1938
when he was elected secretary for the Department
of Evangelism in the Board of Missions of the Methodist Episcopal Church, South. In 1939, with the
formation of The Methodist Church he was named
secretary of the Commission on Evangelism. In 1944,
when the Commission on Evangelism became one
of the major boards of the church, he was named
general secretary of the General Board of Evangelism
of The Methodist Church.* In all of this he was never
out of touch with churches in either the great metropolitan centers or the rural parishes. He was quick
to accept preaching engagements in churches of all
sizes—and he expected the same attitude from his
staff.

As the general secretary of one of the major boards
of the church, he was in close contact with most
of the organization with which the church is concerned. A partial list of the committees on which
he served includes the National Council of Churches,
the World Council of Churches, the World Methodist Council, Council of Secretaries of the Boards and
Agencies, and the Council of Evangelism. In these

* At the time Dr. Denman served, the United Methodist Church had not
yet come into being. The Methodist Church was a unification of the Methodist
Episcopal Church, the Methodist Episcopal Church, South, and the Methodist
Protestant Church.

committees, as elsewhere, he made his presence felt. He was an organizer, a builder—first, last, and all the time, a program man.

If an organization were to forge ahead, be it a church or one of the national boards, he believed that a strong program was always needed. He was a genius at planting ideas for programs in a bishop's mind, then walking away to let them germinate. One day a call would come to him, "Harry, we need some assistance in an undertaking. Would your board be willing to spearhead it?"

To such a request he would give a quick affirmative response and explain to his staff that the bishops "want us to do so and so." His staff would smile knowingly, realizing full well who had been the originator of the program.

"To get anything done in The Methodist Church you must have the bishops behind it," he often said. Always he worked with them, cooperating, encouraging, inspiring, and upon several occasions working behind the scenes as a major figure in having several of them elected to the episcopacy. To him they were always "Bishop." To them he was "Harry." His relationships with them were working relationships, but also spiritual relationships.

It was in this spirit that he almost singlehandedly forged the General Board of Evangelism from one man and a secretary working in a tiny office to an organization of some two hundred fifty persons, with a headquarters building valued àt more than two million dollars. The beautiful Upper Room Chapel with its wood carving of the Last Supper began to attract hundreds of thousands of visitors each year.

One has only to read the pages of Charles Laymon's *Thy Kingdom Come* to see the genius of the man who was the builder.

From the beginning, first as head of a commission and then of a board, Harry Denman moved fast. He rapidly assembled a staff to help him further his programs. He found them and brought them into the organization from different parts of the country and with varied backgrounds. He recruited preachers, businessmen, writers, teachers; and he built the organizational structure, stated its purpose, and welded the various personalities into a team.

Across the years, Harry Denman searched the country, and sometimes other lands, for a person to fit a particular category. Upon occasion he found a person whom he felt might make a contribution; he secured that person and then worked out a suitable assignment.

Always, always, always he had programs to be nurtured, brought to fruitage, and then be replaced by other programs when the first one had run its course. The titles of some of these programs show his vision: the Year of Evangelism, the Crusade for Christ, the Council of Evangelism, the Foundation for Evangelism, the National Lay Committee on Evangelism, the Cooperative Department of Youth Evangelism, the Seventy Evangelists (known as the 70-E) program, the Christmas Conferences, and convocations of evangelism.

With his world mind it was only natural that Harry Denman should think of Missions to America. Persons from other lands were brought to the United States to preach and witness in churches and communities across the nation. These missionaries in reverse came from Argentina, Peru, Africa, India, Burma, the Philippines, Korea, Japan, Hong Kong, and England. This, too, became the responsibility of the General Board staff in cooperation with the Board of Missions as these persons were trained and scheduled across the forty-eight states.

The Board of Evangelism participated in evangelistic missions to special places: Cuba, Hawaii, Alaska, South America, the Orient, India, and Africa. For these missions it was necessary for the Board to recruit persons who could go at their own expense or the expense of their church, to witness and preach.

In the headquarters building there were two publishing units administratively guided by the general secretary. One was The Upper Room. The devotional guide not only increased rapidly to a circulation of some three million copies in thirty-seven languages and Braille, but the section also published hundreds of devotional books and pamphlets.

Tidings and Methodist Evangelistic Materials was responsible for the publication of all training and evangelistic materials and produced hundreds of books, tracts, and other evangelistic helps.

None knew the working of this vast enterprise, even to the most minute detail, better than the general secretary, Harry Denman.

3

NEVER ENOUGH HOURS

Harry Denman was a man with a mandate, a mission, to tell the world about Jesus Christ. He had a wonderful time in a curious, exhausting way. He never seemed to tire of facing an audience or congregation. At the end of a grueling day he could preach for an hour and apparently finish refreshed.

When asked why he never took a vacation, he replied, "I have a vacation all the time. I am enjoying what I am doing so I have a vacation three hundred sixty-five days a year. I am trying to do what I believe the Lord wants me to do."

Those who knew him best often discussed the need for him to take a vacation, but their conclusion was always the same: What would he do? He had no hobbies, no family. He had been everywhere and was going again.

Records show that in one forty-eight-hour period he spoke in five states: Ohio, Michigan, Pennsylvania, Virginia, and Indiana. Two months later, between Monday and Friday noon he spoke in Texas, Mississippi, Kentucky, Georgia, and visited in Alabama and

Pennsylvania. He seemed fired by an inner compulsion that would not let him rest. Like the apostle Paul, he believed that nothing could separate him from the love of Christ—certainly not distance or strange places. And no place was strange to him for very long.

When he arrived in a city or a rural parish to help a pastor with an evangelistic program, he was frequently greeted with the suggestion that after he had rested from his trip perhaps they could sit down together and plan their schedule. His reply was, "Let's go and visit the people. We can plan as we go."

He once defined Christianity as give, give, give. And so he gave of himself unstintingly. When staff members complained of the heavy demands he made on them, they were quick to remind themselves that he always demanded twice as much of himself.

He carried his wardrobe and his office in his briefcase when he traveled. He was ready to go to work wherever he was. Even minutes between planes in a busy airport or while flying were not to be wasted. There were letters to be answered, sermon notes to be written, plans to be outlined, and perhaps a long distance call to be made to his staff in Nashville with more instructions. His mail was forwarded to him every day, as were progress reports of various enterprises and sales reports. It was not unusual for a staff person to receive one, two, or even five memos from him in a day.

He sometimes admitted that perhaps he could do

more work than those of his staff who were married because he did not have family responsibilities. For the most part he was free to make his own schedule which meant trying to jam twenty-six hours into twenty-four and eight days into seven.

Christmas and Thanksgiving were the only two holidays staff could count on. Frequently large out-of-town meetings were planned for the Fourth of July and New Year's, while at the headquarters building it was business as usual on New Year's Day. Labor Day was a good day to work or at least have a staff meeting.

With Harry Denman, thought and action were one. Once he had an idea he could not wait to try it. Halfway through the project he might have another thought which he considered better than the first, and it had to be incorporated immediately. Always thinking, always working, he got ideas as readily at midnight as at noon. Just as quickly he summoned members of his staff.

He once awakened the editor of one of the periodicals at 2 A.M. with the suggestion that the presses be stopped for a change he wanted made in an article he had written. Upon another occasion, after midnight, he called a member of his field staff who was on vacation and said, "I have a speaking engagement in the Bahamas day after tomorrow. I can't make it. I want you to take it for me."

While he had a most efficient business administrator in D. E. Jackson, there was no detail in the management of the fast growing organization with which the general secretary was not conversant.

Over the years as the work grew, there were increased demands for more office and shipping room space, more staff and employees. So there were buildings to be planned and financed, contracts to be negotiated, insurance policies to be considered, and staff members to be hired, trained, or shifted to new areas of responsibility, sometimes at a moment's notice.

Many of these details were handled by letter or telephone while he was out of town preaching, teaching, and witnessing, but the few hours he spent in the office in Nashville were times of feverish activity. To his staff he would often remark, "You'll be glad when I am out of here. Then you can get something done besides answer my questions."

His questions seemed to well up like a spouting geyser. He had an uncanny memory for detail as he digested budget and circulation reports. Why? Why? Why? was the constant question. "Why did you buy this and not this? Have you talked with them at the post office to see if we can't get better service. The letter you mailed on Tuesday didn't reach me until Friday. If it had been mailed an hour earlier would it have made a difference?" Or, "I noticed that we are paying more for wrapping paper this year than we did last. With the quantity we use could we get it cheaper if we went direct to the mills?"

He read all the constant flow of magazines, periodicals, promotion materials, and books being produced by the two editorial departments. To one of his editors he said, "The scripture reference in one of the articles was incorrect. You included one too many verses. The chapter ends with verse 30 not 31 as you indicated. How did all of your proofreaders miss that?"

The schedule he kept while in the office was as unusual as the man himself. Accustomed to missing entire nights of sleep, except for such naps as he might take while he traveled from engagement to engagement, he kept no regular hours except early and late. Sometimes he would retire to his bedroom in the headquarters building at six o'clock in the evening and go to bed immediately, only to get up at midnight and start to work. Six hours is enough sleep for anyone, he often declared. Then while the place was quiet he would have his devotions and spend the rest of the night familiarizing himself with the details of the operation and committee reports, as well as dictating replies to the constant stream of correspondence that came to him.

When leaving the office for the day, his secretarial staff would place a stack of letters on his desk. Next morning they would find that he had dictated replies to all of them as well as many letters to taxi drivers, airline personnel, and hosts and hostesses who had been gracious to him. Many of the letters were to be accompanied by a book he personally had selected.

To a young person he wrote:

> While we were talking last week you asked what is meant by the new birth? I have thought about it

and prayed about it, now finally I am ready to try
to give you an answer.

When you are born a person you have a physical
birth and you love as a person loves which can be
very, very selfish at times. When you are born of the
Lord you have a spiritual birth and you love as God
loves. That is what we call redemptive love. That is
what Jesus did, he lived a redemptive life. He gave
himself.

I am so glad you asked me that question for you
see I needed to think about it.

Please pray for me.

His next letter might be one to a candy manu-
facturer:

Tonight for dessert I had one of your candy bars
for the first time. It was one of the best candy bars
I have ever eaten. I hope more people learn of this
wonderful product and buy it in great quantities.

At the hub of all his activities was Lou Dozier.
For thirty-two years she made the bulk of his travel
arrangements and schedules, handled his personal
finances, and cared for the many details he handed
over to her, which he never looked at again. In
introducing her to friends he said, "Lou knows more
about me than any other person, but don't ask her,
for she won't tell."

Hers was a total dedication, and Harry Denman
could say that because of her attention to detail he
had a freedom which few other executives enjoyed.

Frequently when he was out he would run short of funds. Meeting another staff man, he would borrow whatever that one had available and say, "When you get back to the office tell Lou. She will reimburse you and charge it to me."

Most staff persons, acquainted with the situation, would be quick to say that Lou Dozier played a far greater part in Harry Denman's worldwide ministry than she or others realized.

When Harry Denman was in the office for even a few hours, there developed a series of staff conferences, possibly a full-fledged staff meeting. Christmas week was always a time reserved for staff meetings. At that time churches would be busy with their own programs and have no need of a General Board person. Always there was the interruption of long-distance telephone calls and visitors who "just had to see him."

From time to time he would walk through the building. Stopping by a package wrapper in the shipping room he might ask, "How many packages do you wrap in a day?" Then glancing around he would ask, "Would it be easier for you if the scales were on the other end of the table? I think we should try rearranging the setup out here."

He seemed to enjoy thoroughly having things moved around—sometimes entire departments. For him to spend any length of time in the office often meant the equivalent of playing fruit basket upset. Offices might be moved to a new part of the building. One of his staff remarked, "If Harry had a wife at home to make him move furniture, he wouldn't enjoy it so much at the office."

By evening his suit would be a bit more rumpled, the shoulders of his coat covered with dandruff. His hair, badly in need of the attention of a barber, would look as if he had been out in a high wind. There might be a fresh gravy spot on his black tie, but in the process he would have outlined countless hours of work for his staff, witnessed to visitors in the building, and prayed in the chapel.

There was only one Harry Denman though sometimes it appeared that he was quadruplets.

4

THE FELLOWSHIP
OF THE SHUT DOOR

Many adjectives have been used to describe Harry Denman, but perhaps none more accurately describes him than self-disciplined. Early in life he made a pledge never to feed his body until he had first fed his soul. While he prayed in many places and under the most trying conditions, he followed to the letter Jesus' admonition, "When you pray, go into a room by yourself, shut the door, and pray to your Father who is there in the secret place." And this personal prayer life was reflected in everything he did. Perhaps in a large measure it accounted for his tremendous physical energy.

According to J. Manning Potts, who traveled the world over with him, in 1948 Denman began the unusual practice of copying a portion of the Scriptures every day by longhand into a secretary's notebook. Before his death he had copied all of the New Testament and Psalms and had recopied the Gospels of Mark and John.

Often he would remark to a colleague, "This morning, while I was copying the Scripture, I found a new thought, one that I had never noticed before in my reading."

Copying the scripture, for Harry Denman, was a digestive process. By copying the verses, rather than merely reading them, he felt he could absorb them so completely that they would guide his every thought and action.

Those who heard him preach were almost certain to know the portion of the Bible he was copying, because the words which were so vibrant to him were emphasized in his sermon. They overflowed as a natural expression of what he was finding meaningful for himself. Yet he never confined his time with the Scriptures merely to those morning hours when he was copying them. He read his Testament on the planes, in hotel lobbies, and wherever he had a moment. It was his constant companion.

He used his Testament as a tool to open doors for him so he might witness for his Lord. One time on a plane he saw a person reading a Bible of another language. Taking his own Testament from his pocket he pointed to it, then to the Bible his neighbor was reading. Although they could not communicate verbally, he said they communicated through the spirit, knowing they both worshiped the same God.

In another situation, he went into a small dressing room to disrobe so his suit might be cleaned while he waited. When he emptied his pockets, the attendant noticed his Testament. "Do you carry that with you?" he asked. The attendant immediately went and got his own Bible. There in the tiny dressing room, one man dressed and the other in his shirttail, they prayed together. Writing in the 1968 *Upper Room Disciplines* he said:

> The Master came to fulfill the law and the prophets. He was always quoting Scripture and living it. Jesus revealed to us the discipline of knowing biblical wisdom.
>
> Today we study the Bible. We know who wrote certain books. We know to whom they were written. But do we know their contents? Do we read the Bible devotionally each day? Do we let the Holy Spirit reveal to us the truths of the Scriptures?

Reading the Bible and praying were the warp and woof of Harry Denman's life. Never backward about asking either a person or his Lord to do something, he always sought the Giver before he sought the gift. For him it was the Giver who was precious. And so he could ask the question, "Do we let the Holy Spirit reveal to us the truths of the Scriptures?"

His feelings about prayer were also captured in his writing for the 1968 *Upper Room Disciplines:*

> We need the fellowship of the shut door. This is not a fellowship with persons but with our Father. We are alone with him. We can talk to him and listen to him talk. The fellowship of the shut door is primarily for listening. Sometimes we are so busy petitioning God that we do not give him an opportunity to say to us what he would like for us to hear.
>
> When Paul heard the voice of Jesus calling him he

answered, "What shall I do, Lord?" The Lord told him what to do, and he obeyed.

These are words we should use in our prayer period: "What shall I do, Lord?" This prayer says, "I have accepted your lordship for my life, and I desire to know what you want me to do."

We do not pray, "What do you want the world to do, Lord?"—but, "What shall I do, Lord?" We do not pray, "What do you want the church to do?"—but, "What shall I do, Lord?"

We make this request. We listen. We hear the voice of the living Christ. We say, "Yes." We leave the place of prayer; we obey.

It is the daily discipline of listening to God in the lonely place that will help us obey. If we love God as Jesus loved him we will obey him. We disobey God because we are self-centered and desire to enthrone self. Jesus was God-centered and he enthroned God and crucified that in himself which was opposed to God's will.

Daily prayers of thanksgiving to God lead us to praise God more. Praising him is part of daily devotions. If we have a daily habit of praising our loving heavenly Father, soon we will be praising his children for what they have done for us. Our daily periods of praise will give us gratitude for all the blessings which have come to us from others.

In a letter for the International Prayer Fellowship, he said, "From experience I have learned that when I pray for an individual or a family, or a nation, I fall in love with that person, or that family, or that nation."

Again and again he stressed the importance of listening. "Praying is listening to God," he wrote and preached. "God asks us to do things. We want him to answer our prayers, but do we answer his prayers to us?"

He often used the illustration of talking on the telephone. "When one person does all the talking on the telephone it is not a telephone conversation, it is a monologue. That's what we have with God, a monologue with us doing the talking."

In the same vein Harry Denman often said that while Jesus did not give us many rules about prayer, he did give us a life which demonstrated the power of a disciplined prayer life.

Pointing to the power of prayer and to Jesus' example, he would emphasize that Jesus was praying when he was baptized. Jesus was praying at the time Simon Peter made his great confession. Jesus was praying at the mount of transfiguration and before selecting the twelve. He prayed in the garden while the disciples slept. Always Jesus prayed—morning, noon, and night—but when he could, he went to a solitary place to pray.

And so Harry Denman went to a solitary place to pray, more often than not a hotel or motel room, though it was not only in the morning he prayed. Those who roomed with him soon grew accustomed to returning to their hotel room to find him on his knees beside the bed, often with an open Bible before him.

In his office he kept a kneeling bench which he

used often. Moving quickly from his desk to the kneeling bench he would pray for whatever it was that was occupying his mind. Then as quickly he would return to his desk and continue his dictation.

Early in the morning or late at night when he was in Nashville he liked to go into the Upper Room Chapel and kneel at the altar. Looking up at the beautiful wood carving of the Last Supper, he would pray. If others came in, and often they did, sometimes to pray, but usually to look with rapt attention at the carving, he continued with his prayers. At times they would follow his example and kneel with him. Once when asked if this distracted him he replied, "They don't bother me, and I don't bother them."

While many of his prayers were in secret, there were those who knew something of his prayers. He prayed every day for every bishop in The Methodist Church. He prayed for his staff and their families. He carried the schedule of every staff person with him and would pray for them in their particular situations.

Many times staff members remarked, "Just knowing he was praying for me made the difference."

When prayer requests came to him—and they came by the score—he did not take them lightly. He prayed sincerely and with faith.

Former staff members recall a very desperate situation during the 1956 General Conference in Minneapolis. The conference seemed likely to split asunder over the race issue. The tension mounted. At the close of the day's session, delegates walked from the meeting with heads down and hearts heavy.

Disappointed but not baffled, Harry Denman proposed a solution. Wesley Methodist Church was just down the street from the conference headquarters. Why not have a prayer vigil? He summoned a few others, and they went to the church. They prayed that evening and all during the night. In the words of one who was present, "I shall never forget the raining down of the Holy Ghost the next morning when we came to the auditorium. No more bickering. Harry Denman had prayed."

He was a man who prayed with confidence. We have an example from prayers he wrote for *The Upper Room Disciplines:*

Our Father, we know that you will hear us wherever we are—in the temple or the tabernacle, in the palace or the hut—but help us to have a room where the door is shut and we are alone in the blessed fellowship of praising and listening. Help us to obey the guidance you give us as Jesus did.

Our Father, we thank you for giving us your Son, Jesus Christ. We thank you that we can know him when we obey him. Today, help us to live as he lived. We pray that all persons who see us today will see Christ. Help us to live a surrendered life for the glory of our Savior. We ask this in his dear name and for his sake.

Upon one occasion when asked if he prayed for those whose body had died, he replied, "Of course.

I pray for my mother every day. I ask the Lord to tell her how much I love her. There are so many whose bodies have died for whom I continue to pray. Why not? Their bodies died, but their spirits have gone to join that select company of heaven. Of course I pray for them, just as I hope folks will pray for me when my body has died.

"We believe in the communion of the saints. Isn't prayer communion with the heavenly Father and those who have gone to be with him?"

A longtime friend said, "Harry is a practical mystic. Physically he is in the world, but spiritually he is in that great kingdom we cannot see but can only feel."

While he spent hours in solitary prayer, he liked to go to prayer meetings. He was a member of the Gideons. When he was in a locality where there was a Gideon prayer meeting and he was free to do so, he went.

"I like to hear people pray. I listen to their prayers." Then he would say with a laugh, "It is strange what we ask God to do."

"So many people want to bring God up-to-date. They tell him everything he already knows. There used to be a layman who would pray for me. He would tell God all about my sins. I stopped him one day and told him it was unnecessary for him to do that, for God knew about my sins before he did."

He prayed often in public, but he was quick to point out some of the fallacies of such prayers by remarking, "Too often we pray in order that those in the group will hear what we say."

In attempting to put across his point about listening to God he once asked a group, "Suppose your telephone rings and when you answer a voice says, 'This is the White House, the President wishes to talk with you,' what would you say?"

One man replied, "I would say, 'Wrong number.' "

Denman replied, "When God tries to get us to listen to him, that's what we tell him—that he's got the wrong number."

5

HIS PHILOSOPHY OF EVANGELISM

To sum up Harry Denman's philosophy of evangelism only one word is needed—the word is *love*.

In his report to the annual meeting of the General Board of Evangelism in 1949 he wrote:

> Today the only way one can see love is to see it wrapped up in a person. This is true of faith. The only way we can see Christ is to see him wrapped in a person. Evangelism can only be seen in a person. We need to become a package of love, a package of faith, a package of Christ; then we will be a package of evangelism.

A quarter of a century later he emphasized the same thought in a different way, in a sermon he preached in the Upper Room Chapel. This was after he had retired and had been invited back to speak.

> I am going to read some verses from Paul's letter to the churches at Galatia. "I have been crucified with Christ: the life I now live is not my life, but the life which Christ lives in me; and my present bodily life is lived by faith in the Son of God, who loved me

and sacrificed himself for me. I will not nullify the grace of God; if righteousness comes by law, then Christ died for nothing."

Paul said in the scripture which I read to you, in talking about Jesus, "He loved me." That statement startled me not long ago, and I began to figure out how Paul knew that Jesus loved him. How could he know that Jesus loved him? We say to people now, "You can read it in the Bible," but of course, all that Paul had was the Old Testament. . . .

Now how did Paul know that Jesus loved him? I think he knew it because he saw Stephen. He saw Christ in Stephen. He was present when Stephen was stoned to death. He heard Stephen pray for him when he said, "Do not hold this sin against them." I don't think he could forget that.

Then on the road to Damascus he heard the voice of his Lord speaking to him. Jesus said, "Why do you persecute me?" He didn't say, "Why did you persecute Stephen?" He said, "Why do you persecute me?"

Then Saul prayed a great prayer, "Lord, what wilt Thou have me to do?"

And the Lord told him to arise and go, and his companions led him to Damascus. He was going there as a conqueror, but now he went as a blind prisoner of the Lord Jesus Christ. I think he felt the love of Christ when Jesus spoke to him on the road to Damascus.

In Damascus there came a man to see him one day and he said, "Brother Saul." I think those are two of the sweetest words in the English language, "Brother Saul." He had gone to Damascus to capture this man and take him back to Jerusalem, but this man, by the love of Christ, captured him. "Brother Saul, the same Lord who appeared to you on the road to Damascus appeared unto me and told me to come and put my hands upon you that you might receive your sight and be filled with the Holy Spirit."

In Paul's letter to the church at Galatia he says he went to Arabia. Three years later, after his experience under the leadership of Ananias, he went to Jerusalem, and the church would not receive him.

The church can be rather mean at times. The church wouldn't receive Gandhi because of his color. Maybe Gandhi would have been a great Christian. We don't know. He certainly lived the gospel of Jesus Christ. He lived it. When his body died the newspaper said, "He lived what we say with our lips." He accepted the teachings of Jesus Christ. We don't. We say we believe in him, but we don't accept him or his teachings.

So the church in Jerusalem would not receive Paul because of his persecution, but there was a man by the name of Barnabas. He took him by the hand and took him to the apostles and told them what had happened, and they received him.

Paul saw the love of Christ in Barnabas. . . .

Paul had fellowship with the church until he got in an argument, disputing with the Jews who spoke Greek, and they wanted to kill him. I think he saw the love of Christ in the Christian church in Jerusalem, because they took him out of town and down to Caesarea, then sent him off to Tarsus.

In the meantime there was a great spiritual awakening down at Antioch in Syria, and the apostles sent Barnabas down there. When he saw what was going on he knew he had to have help so he went to Tarsus, found Paul, and took him to Antioch. These two men taught the people there for a year, and they were called *Christian* for the first time at Antioch.

He saw the love of Christ in Barnabas. Naturally he knew that Christ loved him, but because he saw the love of Christ in people it meant more to him.

Love has to be seen. I am not very sympathetic with the idea of telling people that God loves them. I don't know why so many people are doing it today. They come up and say, "God loves you." It has to be seen.

I used to think if I had plenty of money I would put up billboards all over the United States saying, "God Loves You," but one day in Korea the Lord said, "You don't have to put up billboards. You are a billboard. Every Christian is a billboard."

If people do not see the love of Christ in us, I am not sure that we are followers of Christ. I am not sure we know him. . . .

It is nice to say we love Jesus. It is nice to say, but it is so hard to keep his commandments. "This is my commandment: love one another, as I have loved you."

He showed us his love for us by the way he lived. The glorious thing about Jesus was that he thought more of persons than he did of property. He said that children are the greatest. I wish The Methodist Church believed children are the greatest.

There are certain churches today that are using buses. I get bulletins saying a certain church is busing hundreds of people to church. Now I have an idea of what I would like to see done. The more people you bus to church the more buildings you have to put up. When you buy a bus you have to put up a building. Now what I would like to see us do is to buy double-decker buses and go out into the communities where the mobile homes are, the ghettos, and the inner city. Let the young people be the teachers. Take the young people out there to teach the children and the teen-agers on Sunday and during the week. I want the church to be in the bus business rather than in the building business. That's the way to reach people.

Over and over again he emphasized, "If the church is to survive, the church must want people. It must make people welcome. It must love people."

Frequently he would refer to the years he was associated with Arthur J. Moore (later to become a bishop) at the First Methodist Church in Birmingham, Alabama. He said:

I learned the importance of evangelism from him. He believed that the Sunday school was the best place to emphasize this. Every Sunday morning he stood at the main door of the educational building and shook hands with everyone who came: men, women, youth, and children. Every Sunday during Lent he would speak to a different Sunday school class. He told them about Christ and gave the invitation.

Dr. Moore was a ritualist. He gave the invitation to accept Christ as Savior and unite with the church every Sunday. He believed in following the order of worship in the ritual. There are three orders of worship, and all of them have listed the invitation to Christian discipleship. The ritualist is an evangelist.

Our business as Christians is to extend the invitation

to all persons by the way we live and by word of mouth. We are witnesses for Christ who desires that we have life.

Years ago I saw the love of Christ in a man who used to come to church every Sunday morning and every Sunday night. He was deaf. He never heard a sermon, he never heard the choir sing, but he sat there twice every Sunday. He was a Moravian. There was not a Moravian church in our city so he belonged to our church. Every summer he went to Colorado for his vacation. Every Easter he went to Winston-Salem for the great Moravian service on Easter morning. He lived in a commodious house. He was very liberal to the church. He gave to all the special causes. Then the depression came. He eliminated the trip to Colorado. He eliminated the trip to Winston-Salem. He eliminated the house in which he lived and moved to a smaller one. Every Monday morning I would look at his envelope because that was my job. He never cut his giving to the church. He never cut his giving to all the special causes. In him I saw the love of Christ.

The love of Christ has to be seen. People talk about how they love the church, but they put things of this world ahead of the church. He didn't.

Earlier this year I went to Birmingham to help in the coronation service of a woman I loved dearly because she loved me. She was a lovely woman, and her daughters were the queens in the great balls that society gave every year. She could have run the town socially with her wealth, her culture, and education. She belonged to the most exclusive literary club in the city, but she taught a Sunday school class. I would go visiting with her. Our church was right in the rooming house section, a great place for a church to be. That is where the church ought to be today.

As we went to see these dear old women who ran the rooming houses, she would kiss them. I would ask, "Why in the world do you like to kiss these old women?" She would reply, "It doesn't hurt me and they like it."

Some two or three months after my mother went to heaven, I went to Duke University to teach in a pastors' school. I was living in a hotel, for I had moved there from the home I shared with my mother. When I came back to that hotel from the pastors' school, I thought I was in the wrong room. That woman had gone to the hotel and put up curtains and pictures. It was a home for me. That hotel room became a home because she had made it a home, attractive and beautiful, and I saw Christ in her. I loved her and she loved me.

When I was in the hospital I got a note every morning from a couple. They loved me dearly and I loved them. I saw Christ.

Write a love letter to somebody, maybe a teacher you had when you were a child, maybe a preacher who helped you when you were in your teens. Write a letter thanking someone. Let that one see the love of Christ in you. It may mean the conversion of somebody like Saul of Tarsus. You never know.

6

THE FISHERMAN

THE CRAGGY-BROWED man in a rumpled suit, often with holes in his shoes but with a twinkle in his eyes, seldom missed an opportunity to witness and pray with anyone, anytime, anywhere. In a self-imposed parish that encompassed the world, this fisherman for souls shared with bartenders and porters, airline pilots and housewives, boys and girls. He talked with them about their personal relationship to God.

He was particularly at home with taxi drivers. Sliding into the front seat with one he would begin by asking, "My brother, tell me about your family?" Then after listening, perhaps viewing a snapshot hastily pulled from a billfold, he would ask, "Where do they go to church?" Once that fact was established he would almost invariably ask, "Who is the preacher?" Or in the case of a Roman Catholic, "Who is the priest?"

Most generally the driver could make the connection, though there might be a bit of fumbling at that point. Then the next question would be, "With this job do you have much chance to go to church with your family?"

And the usual reply was, "Not too often."

Undaunted by this response the follow-up question was, "I'll bet you pray?"

"Yes. Probably not as much as I should."

"None of us do, my brother. But will you pray for me?"

In Kansas City, while being taken from the airport to the church where he was speaking, Harry Denman began asking the usual questions of the taxi driver. The driver said he was no longer living with his family. He said he had had a drinking problem and his wife had taken the children and left the city.

"Do you still have that problem?"

"I haven't had a drink for six months," the driver responded.

"Does your wife know that?"

"No. She probably wouldn't believe me if I told her."

"Maybe someone else could tell her," Harry Denman suggested.

The driver looked closely at him. "How long will you be at this church?" When told of the approximate time he said, "I'll be here waiting for you."

When Dr. Denman came out, true to his word the driver was there. As they drove back to the airport, the conversation was resumed. Suddenly the driver asked, "Would you be willing to write my wife and tell her of our conversation? I'll give you her address."

He was assured that such a letter would be given top priority; they had a brief prayer together, and the evangelist was on his way to keep another engagement.

"What we need to do is to get people to pray," this personal evangelist would tell his colleagues. "I always try to get people to pray for something, even for me. If they can pray for me they can pray for lots of other things, even themselves."

While he had implicit belief in the power of prayer, he was never content to settle for prayer alone. Once when speaking to a group of women in a local church he was told that a prostitute lived nearby. "What have you done about it?" he asked.

"We are praying for her," he was told.

"But have you gone to call on her? Have you told her that God loves her and that you love her?"

There was a long silence.

Later, in relating the incident he said, with one of his quick laughs, "That's just the trouble. Too often we try to substitute prayer for action. We want the Lord to do what we are not willing to do ourselves."

A bishop said, "Harry Denman can ask a waitress in a restaurant about her spiritual life more easily than many preachers can raise the question in the privacy of a member's home."

And that was very true. Former staff members recall being in Illinois for an evangelistic meeting. One Sunday morning several of them, with their leader, went to a local restaurant for breakfast. When

the waitress came to their table to take the order,
Harry Denman remarked about the wedding band
she was wearing. Then he inquired about her family.
When told she had a husband and a baby daughter,
he asked where they went to church. She gave the
name of the church where they had their membership, but added that because of her work on Sunday
they were unable to attend.

"Have you had your daughter baptized?" Harry
Denman asked.

"We want to, but because of my work we haven't
been able to make those arrangements," she replied.

"But do you want to have her baptized?"

"Oh, yes. We want to give her a Christian home
and Christian training."

For the evangelist that was enough to go ahead.
Before he left the restaurant that morning he had
talked with the owner and arranged for the waitress
to have the next Sunday off to have the baby baptized.

Some of these occasions were not without their
humor. Once he asked a waitress, who was serving
his breakfast, if she would pray for him. She regarded
him for a moment, then with a sly grin asked, "What
were you up to last night?"

Perhaps the thing that sparked his quick approach
to witnessing was an incident that happened in Mississippi early in his national ministry. Of that incident
he wrote:

I was staying in a hotel. The day clerk was very
kind to me. The Lord put it on my heart to speak

to him about being a Christian. I did not know whether or not he was a Christian. I told the Lord I would do it, but not at that time because there were many people in the lobby.

Two mornings later I came down to the dining room for breakfast. The night clerk was on duty. The day clerk was supposed to be there. After breakfast the night clerk was still on duty. I inquired about the day clerk. He said, "We found him dead in his room this morning. He used a gun." I went to my room and begged God for forgiveness. I was trying to have a revival, and I failed God and this man who had been gracious to me.

In the years to come he never thought about persons as being either good or bad. He saw every person as one whom Christ loves, and every sinner in the light of who he or she might become. For him to share his love for Christ and his fellow human beings was as natural as breathing, and just as necessary for spiritual survival. In good weather and bad he walked the back country roads in rural communities or the alleys and streets in cities looking for those with whom he might share his Christian witness. In other countries where he did not speak the language, he used an interpreter. Often he visited those living in dire poverty. Through the interpreter he would ask about the person's health, find something in the home to comment upon, but always he would talk about Jesus Christ and his great love. There would be a simple prayer, a smile, and a handclasp; then he would go on to the next place.

In visitation he made it a practice to witness to children. "Children are persons," he said. He told this story:

One night I was in the city of Chicago engaged in evangelistic visiting in the homes of people. My teammate and I called on a family. We gave our witness to the father. He replied negatively. His wife did the same. We were leaving the home when the teenage son of the family came in. I gave the witness about Christ to him. He also replied negatively. Again we were leaving the house when the daughter, who was twelve or thirteen years of age, spoke to me and said, "I wish to become a Christian." We had overlooked her. We witnessed to her, and she made her commitment to Christ and the church. I apologized to her for my failure to recognize her and asked God to forgive me.

He once said all the bootleggers in town came to his mother's coronation service. He treasured their friendship, and they treasured his, even knowing he was a liquor-hating man. They realized he loved them for their souls and that he would work unceasingly to get them to change their ways.

Billy Graham once called him, "The greatest practitioner of personal evangelism in America."

"All I have done is what those of us are supposed to do who are Christians," Harry Denman explained. "This thing of being a Christian is to be concerned about people."

His concern for people was evidenced clearly

when he arrived in a strange community for any length of time. His first approach was to ask pastors for the names of those who were not attending church. In one way or another he found an opening to visit with them, to pray with them, and to invite them to church, not necessarily the church where he was preaching, but to the church or synagogue where they would feel most at home.

"Of course I go into the bars and liquor stores," he replied when questioned about the matter. "They need to know that God loves them the same as anybody else. I just tell them I'd like to visit with them for a few minutes and invite them to come to church. Folks are willing to talk if they think you are sincere. If there is an opportunity I pray, first for the country, then for them. I ask them to pray for me."

With a sharply critical tone he often said, "So often we church people look down our noses when someone does something of which we disapprove. We just hug ourselves a little tighter and think how wonderful we are. Of course there are many things which we cannot approve, but if we are true to Jesus' command we still must love the person."

He was never an ordained minister. A newspaper reporter characterized him as "one who guards his layman's standing the way an athlete does his amateur rank." And he truly felt that he could be of more useful service to God's kingdom as a layman than he could as an ordained minister.

He emphatically believed that every Christian was

obligated to be a priest, a missionary, an evangelist. "There's too much letting the preacher do it," he often said. "We must have the same concern for persons Christ had. The church has got to leave the pew and go to the people in the home, the shop, the fields. It's our actions that speak, not what we say."

He demonstrated this well one morning when he passed a home next door to a church. A man was sitting in a wheelchair on the porch. One leg was missing. Walking up the front walk, Harry Denman said, "Good morning, my brother."

The salutation startled the man, and he replied, "You're the first man who ever called me brother."

Ignoring the sharpness of the tone, Harry Denman said, "Tell me, how did you lose your leg?"

That opened the flood gates. Everyone likes to talk about his or her operation, and that man proved to be no exception.

In a matter of minutes they were talking together, then praying. Then came the usual followup, an invitation to church. The man smiled a slow, sad smile. "I've lived next door to the church for years, and no one has ever asked me to come. No one has ever called me brother until you did today." He reached in his pocket and took out a twenty dollar bill. "This is for you," he said.

Harry Denman refused. But in telling of the incident later he said, "Probably he thought I needed it to get my suit cleaned."

For other people, the holidays were a time to relax

from the press of normal duties, but Harry did not relax from witnessing. Christmas was the day for him to share with those behind prison bars.

According to friends this custom began one Christmas morning while he was on the staff of the First Methodist Church in Birmingham. He telephoned the warden of the city jail whom he had come to know and said, "I'd like to be admitted to the main block of the prison and share the day with those who are in there."

The surprised warden protested, "No provision has been made for any religious services today."

"I don't want to preach. I only wish to eat Christmas dinner with the men."

His friend the warden continued to protest, "Harry, you can't really mean that."

"Why not? Just bring me a pan of food like the rest."

Not only did he go there, but in the evening he went to the county jail and had his evening meal with the prisoners there.

The experience not only became a habit with him while he was in Birmingham, but it was one he continued after he became the general secretary of the General Board of Evangelism. He would refuse invitations to the homes of his staff members on Christmas Day. Instead he would eat with the prisoners in the state penitentiary, the county jail, or the workhouse—wherever he could be admitted most readily.

Upon more than one occasion, while conducting

services in a beautiful sanctuary he would startle the pastor and congregation by remarking, "We have had a great spiritual blessing here, now let's go to the jail and visit the folks there. They need our prayers and love."

Before they realized what was happening, some surprised folks found themselves on the way to the jail to witness in a fashion they never dreamed possible.

During an interview with Harry Denman, United Press International writer Louis Cassels asked if the average housewife or businessman could do the type of witnessing he did. Harry Denman replied: "Yes, anyone can do it if he tries. It's like jumping under a cold shower. After you get under it's all right."

He continued, "There are many ways of doing it. It is easier, usually, to start with someone you know. If you have new neighbors and notice they stay at home on Sunday morning, you have an opening to invite them to go to your church with you. They may accept your invitation, or they may tell you that they do not believe in going to church. Either way you have a chance to talk with them about Christ.

"Maybe you have a friend or business associate who is in trouble. Help in any concrete way that you can, and meanwhile watch for the right moment to tell where you turn for strength and courage when you are in trouble."

Asked if people resent a witness as an intrusion in their personal affairs he replied, "I have talked with a good many thousands of people, and I have never met one who resented it. You cannot do this kind of thing unless you really care for people. They can always tell. If you are trying to get an A on your own spiritual report card instead of trying to help someone else find Christ, you'll fail."

Asked if a casual conversation can convert a non-Christian, he replied, "No. What you are trying to do is plant the seed. Many seeds may fall on rocky ground. But some will take root. A word from you at the right moment may be just the little push that is needed to change an entire life. I would rather say a million words that did no good than to leave unsaid the one or two that could have been crucial. Remember, you are never asked to do the work alone; God is working on the project too."

At the age of eighty, while speaking in Dallas, Texas, Harry Denman was still hammering away at his theme—the need to visit. He was worrying whether The United Methodist Church would be around by the year 2000 if membership figures continued to dip. He said, "We can study more books and do less than any crowd I know. Our trouble is we don't believe people need Jesus Christ. But I still look to him for the answer. The great thing about Jesus is that he didn't have any committee. He didn't have any organization. He had time to visit."

Harry Denman's parents.
Hattie Leonard Denman and
William Henry Denman.
Birmingham, Alabama,
January, 1893.

Harry Denman

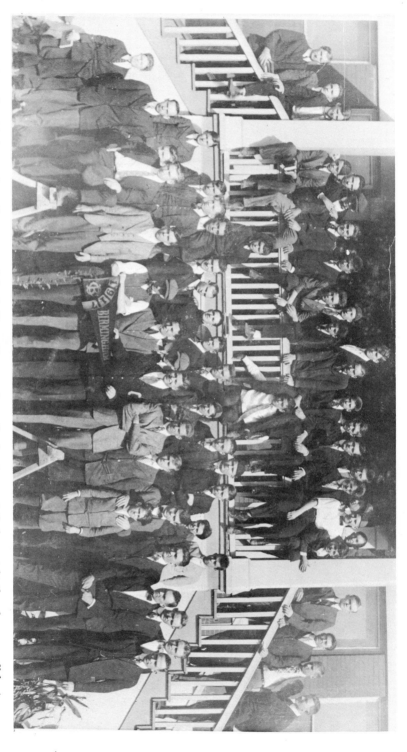

Class of 1917, Birmingham Preparatory School. Harry Denman is on the front row, sixth from right (hands on small boy).

Graduation class, 1921, Birmingham-Southern College. (l. to r.) W. G. Barnes, Dana White, Albert L. Branscomb, Stanley L. Morgan, Annie Lee Warren, Waymon P. Snuggs, S. M. Baker, Fred Sparks, Jesse R. Duncan, Harry Denman; (in car) Susie Rosamond Plan, Mary Hunter, Joe M. Neese.

February, 1946. Atlantic City, New Jersey. Addressing the committee of 200 which managed the Crusade for Christ of The Methodist Church. Bishop J. Ralph Magee presiding.

Harry Denman and Dr. George Truman Carl at the conclusion of Dr. Denman's address to the 87th annual summer assembly, Methodist Campground, Des Plaines, Illinois. July, 1946.

John Q. Schisler, Executive Secretary, General Board of Education, and Harry Denman at annual meeting of General Board of Evangelism, Cincinnati, Ohio. January 17, 1950.

In Cuba, commenting on reports of the evangelistic crusade. 1954.

Sharing in the street preaching program. Bloomington, Illinois. 1954.

Tent preaching, 1955.

Harry Denman and Bishop W. Angie Smith with the Warner Sallman portrait of Denman presented at the Board of Evangelism meeting. 1964.

April, 1958. Dedication of the new headquarters building and the Upper Room Chapel. (l. to r.) Bishop W. Angie Smith, Bishop Odd Hagen, Bishop Roy H. Short, Harry Denman, J. Manning Potts.

Harry Denman and his staff, 1951. (l. to r.) George H. Jones, Howard W. Ellis, Harold L. Hermann, G. Ernest Thomas, Dawson C. Bryan, D. E. Jackson, Harry Denman, C. Lloyd Daugherty, Jr., Harry L. Williams, Joseph H. Edge, J. Manning Potts, J. W. Golden.

(above) 1971.

(left)

May, 1962. Leaving the Nashville office.

7

HE LIVED TO PREACH

W HEN TELLING of being asked by the bishops to
leave his position as business manager of a church
in Birmingham and take a place in the general
church, Harry Denman said, "I told them that I was
not an ordained man, that I did not even have a
license to preach; but Bishop Paul Kern spoke up
and said, 'Harry, you can make a little talk.' " With
a smile Harry Denman added, "That's what I've been
doing ever since, just making little talks."

While there were many little talks, there were
also many major addresses to general conferences,
jurisdictional conferences, annual conferences, national and international convocations. All who listened soon knew that Harry Denman lived to preach.
A long-time friend once said, "If Harry could drop
dead in the pulpit he would die happy."

A born preacher, he was a master at getting and
holding audience attention and inviting partici-
pation. He had learned his craft from some of the
best pulpiteers of his day; yet never was he an imita-
tor. In the pulpit, as elsewhere, he was a unique

individual with his own techniques, sometimes breaking every rule in the book as taught in public speaking, but always moving his audience in the direction he wanted them moved. The change of voice from a rumbling bass to a squeaky falsetto, striking the pulpit with the flat of his hand until it sounded like a splitting board, the fierce frown, the jutting underlip, the short, quick laugh, the sharp incisive question, the pungent story, the pause—he used them all.

Never without his New Testament, from which he read frequently during the average sermon, he once managed midway through a sermon to involve the congregation in a frantic hunt for it. He had already read from it a couple of times; but when he reached for it again, seemingly it had disappeared. "Now where did I put it?" he demanded, searching through the pockets of his coat and ragged sweater. "I had it just a minute ago. All of you saw that. Nobody has been up here to take it."

"It is in your inside coat pocket, Harry," the host pastor suggested.

"No, it isn't. That's the first place I looked."

"You put it in your sweater pocket," a woman in the front pew said.

"I wouldn't put it there. I've got a hole in that pocket," he replied.

"Probably it fell on the floor," the organist said.

Glancing downward he replied, "It's not there. Well, we'll just stop until we find it." Then with a roguish grin he pulled it from his hip pocket. "What do you know, I never put it there before. That's what happens when you get old." But he had their attention, and they loved it.

Years after he had preached on a college campus, the pastor of a church in another denomination wrote: "I can remember as a college student listening to you. Your devotion to Christ and your austere life-style has always been an inspiration to me."

Even with the wildest guess, there is no way for anyone to estimate the number of times he preached, let alone the thousands upon thousands who heard him and felt their lives were changed as a result.

A banker said, "When I first saw him walk up to the pulpit I thought he had nothing for me, but before he had been speaking long I forgot all about how he looked and was sitting on the edge of the pew listening."

He liked especially to preach or talk with young people, and they flocked to him. He never talked down to them. He held out the challenge of what they might become, even when he was most critical of them.

Never was his preaching confined to the pulpit. Sharing the word was in his letters, in his staff meetings, in the articles and meditations he wrote. It had a way of getting into even the most casual conversation. It was as much a part of him as breathing. Because of his naturalness it was more of a personal visit than preaching for many persons though they might be one of hundreds in the congregation.

His sermons were always Bible centered and Christ

centered, but he had a quick way of fitting them to the moment. He seldom preached the same sermon twice because new ideas were always popping up. There were certain themes and phrases that kept reoccurring: *The Word became flesh; Obedience; God first, others second, self last.*

Time after time he would say, "Jesus chose God instead of self. The person who lives for self is lost. It is self that destroys us."

Pointing to Jesus as the example, he would say:

Jesus had many choices. See how he made them. He took a person instead of property. He took God instead of self. He came to minister instead of having others minister to him. He took a towel and a basin. He took a child instead of the rich young ruler. Of course he loved the rich young ruler, but the rich young ruler loved self.

Jesus sought the unsought. He loved the unlovely. He wanted the unwanted. He came not to judge but to save. Jesus came to make love known, and when he left the earth in the flesh he sent the Holy Spirit to give us the power to love all persons.

Perhaps his greatest theme was love. He often told the story of the woman taken in adultery. He said:

The doctors of the law brought a sinful woman to Jesus, the son of love. They desired to test him. The King James translation says, "But Jesus stooped down, and with his finger wrote on the ground, as though he heard them not." Jesus tried to ignore them. This is the way love behaves. Love does not care to hear gossip or scandal about persons.

Love (Jesus) said to those religious men who had brought the sinning woman to him, "The one of you who is faultless shall throw the first stone." It seems that he is saying we will keep the law of Moses, but those who are to do the stoning shall be without sin. That statement eliminated the religious teachers. They went away one by one. Love (Jesus) is left alone with the woman. Love does not throw stones. Love said, "You may go. I do not condemn you, but do not sin again."

I think when she returned to her friends they asked her, "What did the young rabbi from Galilee say to you?" She said, "He did not condemn me, but he told me not to do it anymore." And in my imagination I hope she said, "And I will not." I believe she responded to the kindness of Love (Jesus).

Jesus was the only one who could have thrown a stone that day, but he threw love. Those of us who do wrong do not want stones thrown at us.

Think how kind Jesus was to this woman. Love does not condemn, but love is loving the condemned. Love is stronger than condemnation. Children respond to commendation more than condemnation.

Jesus loved a thief. He took a thief with him to paradise.

What makes a person valuable? God's love.

At times this lay preacher used satire and used it effectively. In a pastors' school where there had been considerable theological debate and little talk of evangelism, Harry Denman rose to speak. Turning

in his Testament to the eighth chapter of Acts, he
read the story of Philip going to the Ethiopian eu-
nuch. "Now this man was trying to understand the
scriptures—Isaiah. Well, the first thing Philip did
was to tell him there were two Isaiahs. That made
everything all right."

When the laughter had died down he continued.
"I don't think Philip knew whether there were two
Isaiahs or one, but he knew about the love of Jesus
Christ. When Philip witnessed to that man, he
wanted to be baptized. They came to some water.
Philip baptized this man who was searching desper-
ately for something he did not have, but wanted—the
love of God."

In 1938 something of these same themes appear
in a sermon he preached to the General Conference
of the Methodist Episcopal Church, South, urging
union with the Methodist Episcopal Church and the
Methodist Protestant Church.

I stand here today to plead for union because in
the name of our Christ and our church we can go
into every American city, into every American village,
into every American town, out on the roadside and
preach the gospel to thousands who need the gospel
today. I do not want a united church that is going
to be institutionalized, but I want a church that is
going to be on fire for Jesus Christ.

You remember after the days of the great blessing
of Pentecost that one day Peter, the rugged fisherman
of Galilee, and John, the Son of Thunder, went to the

Temple to pray. One was impetuous, one was a mystic; one would use the sword, and the other would use love; but after Pentecost they were brothers and worked together.

They reached the Beautiful Gate and there was lame humanity waiting for them. Peter said, "Silver and gold have I none; but such as I have give I thee: In the name of Jesus Christ of Nazareth rise up and walk," and the lame man went into the Temple praising God.

Today, lame humanity sits at the doors of our temples asking for alms. Are we going to toss a nickel or dime into the beggar's hand, or are we together, like Peter and John, in the name of the risen Christ with the power of Pentecost in our hearts, going to give to lame humanity all that it needs physically, and all that it needs spiritually?

My brethren, I am confident of one thing, America will never be healed with all the panaceas we may prescribe until we ourselves have Pentecost and then go into the highways and hedges, into the shops and gutters, into the slums and country byways and say, "In the name of Jesus of Nazareth, arise and walk."

Seldom, if ever, did Harry Denman preach that he did not give an invitation for a Christian commitment. This invitation was always in his own unique way. From an unnamed writer here is such a description.

"It was revival time at Indian Springs Camp Meeting. I was attending as part of a youth group. Dr. Harry Denman was the featured speaker. He was powerful and persuasive in the preaching of the gospel and greatly influenced my decision to pursue the Christian ministry as my life's goal.

"At the close of the evening's service, Dr. Denman gave the invitation. He asked those who were moved by the Spirit to give their lives to Jesus Christ to come forward. A young man standing next to me had never made this step, and I could see that he wanted to respond. As we sang the last stanza of the hymn I nudged his arm and we walked to the mourner's bench together.

"My friend knelt there and with anguish of soul expressed his desire to be able to dedicate his entire being to the Master. The service ended, but he remained. He had not found what he was seeking. Dr. Denman came down from the platform to talk with him. He asked the boy questions about himself, his family, and his church background. He urged him to surrender all and to be at peace with God. Then he led in prayer.

"The prayer ended and Dr. Denman said to my friend, 'Has anything happened? Have you found what you are searching for?' Each question was answered by a rapid shaking of the head. Finally Dr. Denman said to the boy, 'Open your eyes and look at this bench. Do you see the crack running down the bench?' An affirmative answer was indicated by a nodding of the head. 'Now,' said Dr. Denman, 'let us say that this side of the crack, the side where you are, is the devil's side, and this side of the crack, the side where I happen to be is the Lord's side. Do you understand?' Again there was a nodding of the head. 'Fine,' said Dr. Denman, 'Now what are you going to do about it?'

"For a long time my friend gazed at that crack while we waited. Suddenly he got up and jumped over the bench and cried out, 'Now I'm on the Lord's side!'"

8

MATERIALISM

A RECURRING THEME in Harry Denman's preaching and writing was materialism. He knew the story of the rich young ruler so well he often paraphrased it in his own words without opening his Testament. One sermon ran like this:

A young man came to see Jesus one day. This young man was very rich, and he said he would like to have life. Jesus said to him, "Thou knowest the Ten Commandments," and the man replied he had done all that. Then Jesus said, "Go sell what you have and give it to the poor, and put your trust in things in heaven, and take up your cross and follow me."

And the young man said, "No." He said no to the spiritual and yes to the material. The Bible says he had great possessions, but possessions had him. There is nothing wrong in having the material as long as you have it, but when the material has you is when trouble comes. We are possessed with the material instead of the spiritual.

There was a man with a big farm. He raised some great crops. Then he began to worry and ask, "What am I going to do with it all?" But he had an idea. He would just build some more barns. He wanted to keep it all for himself. So he kept on building barns and building barns and building barns until all of his barns were full. Finally he was satisfied so he said, "Soul, take your ease. You have all the good things you need for many years to come."

But our Lord said, "Thou fool, this night your soul shall be required of you. Then whose things shall these be, all the stuff you have in the barns?"

Jesus called him a fool because he tried to feed his soul with the things you put in a barn, but you can never do that. Strange how the people of America are trying to feed their souls with the stuff you put in a barn.

"Today many of us are trying to find life in material possessions rather than by accepting the call of Jesus," he wrote in *The Upper Room Disciplines* (1962). "Jesus says to all—Galilieans, Samaritans, publicans, Pharisees, the educated, the illiterate, all classes and races—'Come ye after me, and I will make you to become. . . .' If we meet the conditions, we will become what he desires us to become and not what we desire to become."

In *Disciplines* (1962) he also wrote:

I saw at Oberammergau the agony of Judas as it was enacted on the stage. Judas knew the spiritual, but he yielded to the material. I saw the agony of Simon Peter, who knew Christ but yielded to social pressure. I saw the agony of Pilate, who knew the truth that Jesus was innocent but yielded to political pressure. I saw the agony of Caiaphas, who knew God but yielded to the institution. I saw the agony of Jesus as he cried in the Garden of Gethsemane, "O my Father, if it be possible, let this cup pass from me; nevertheless not as I will, but as thou wilt." He knew the will of God for him, and he yielded to it.

Judas, Simon Peter, Pilate, and Caiaphas give us a picture of our lives. We yield to the pressure of the material, the social, the political, the institutional. But we must be like Jesus and be obedient to the will of God for our lives.

When questioned about the austerity of his lifestyle, Harry Denman often remarked, "It is fun to see how little one can live on. Not having to keep up with the Joneses takes away much of the strain."

He did not believe it was wrong to have material possessions, but he did believe it was wrong to let the material possess you. "The Christian knows that material possessions are for the glory of God and the services of man. At death we are forced to leave it all behind. We are only stewards. God is the absolute owner," he preached over and over again.

Preaching to members of an annual conference he thundered, "Some of you kneel in front of your safety deposit boxes instead of at the altar." With perspiration streaming from his face and soaking his already wilted shirt collar, he shouted:

Why don't you open them up and give some away? Then you won't have to worry about it. You don't have to be rich to worship material things. Some people can worship even a few dollars. Jesus said to pile up treasures in heaven. Of course, we don't take Jesus seriously. He had only one robe and no place to lay his head. In some countries where I travel I see whole families sleeping out on the sidewalk in the rain. Here on a cold night we just turn up our electric blankets.

In some places I go, the people know how to walk. To own a bicycle is a luxury. In this country we have two cars and a boat. Our two major problems are parking space and reducing. Maybe if we walked more we wouldn't have to worry about either.

Look what we spend on cosmetics, tobacco, and liquor.

I asked one woman what it cost to feed her dog. When she told me I said, "That's more than some families in the world spend for food." Maybe she was just putting me on, wanted to hear what I would say, for she added, "That's not all. I have to take him to be clipped and have his toenails trimmed. Then I have to have his teeth cleaned."

Changing his voice to a falsetto he continued:

Imagine that for a dog? Wouldn't it be nice to be a dog instead of a baby starving to death?

With half the world going to bed hungry at night we're spending fortunes learning how to reduce. I get so tired of articles about reducing—new diets. All we need to do is stop eating so much. It hurts to be hungry. That's what we need to do, hurt a little.

When Jesus saw hungry people, he fed them. He

and his disciples didn't eat it all themselves. They shared what they had, a few loaves and some fish, and there was some left over. We have some left over, but we put it in our garbage cans.

In his papers there was an article he had written under the title, "Yesterday—Today—Tomorrow." He wrote:

We carry in our pockets a piece of paper which has printed on it four great words, "In God we trust." Is that a fact, or is it fiction?

On Sunday in God's house we say, "I believe in God," four great words. How do we behave? Does our behavior reveal our belief, or do we live for self and for the material?

At our clubs and schools and civic meetings we pledge our allegiance to the flag of our nation and say, "One nation under God." Four great words. Is it? Or is it under the domination of selfish interests and political parties?

We say in the pledge of allegiance, "Liberty . . . justice for all." Four great words. Do we want all persons to have liberty or just a few? Do we want all persons including ourselves to have justice?

If this nation is to live, then the four great words must become flesh in you and me. God must be seen in our daily living. Liberty and justice must be seen in our daily living.

What is God? God is love, not cheap sentimental love, but redeeming love which cannot be said but must be seen in the way we live.

Not only did this outspoken critic of waste and materialism preach the philosophy of doing and sharing, he lived it. For him there was no desire for material possessions personally, but for his Lord's church and God's children he did covet the wealth of the nation that others might be fed physically as well as spiritually.

Because he had experienced the hurts of poverty first hand, he could go with sympathy and understanding to the aid of those who were suffering from want.

Added to his own personal knowledge of poverty, he experienced it in the lives of those around him during the great depressions in the late twenties and thirties. In the industrial city of Birmingham it is reported that more than one out of every three persons were on public relief rolls.

Acquaintances during those depression days tell how a doctor would call Harry Denman, who was then on the staff of the First Methodist Church, and say, "I just left a prescription at the home of one of your members. I know they don't have the money to get it filled."

Somewhere this benefactor to whom so many turned would find the necessary money and rush to the aid of the one in need.

It is said by those who remember that frequently at the end of the day he had given away every cent in the benevolent treasury of the church and all he had in his own pockets. Across the years this was a characteristic of his that became a full grown passion. His letter files are filled with testimonies and notes of appreciation from those he helped at a time in their lives when the crisis was greatest. This was the biggest legacy he left for those who remember.

9

ONLY ONE SUIT

Harry Denman might well have been the inspiration for the song, "I've got only one suit, that's all I can wear."

Sometimes when he invited a person to go to church, the other replied, "I'm not dressed good enough to go to church."

The quick answer was always, "Look at me. You're dressed as good as I am."

Returning from a trip around the world, he startled customs inspectors by presenting only one opened briefcase for examination. "Where's the rest of your baggage?" the inspector asked.

"That's it," the world traveler replied.

"But I mean the things you checked, those you took with you, and what you bought while you were gone," the inspector persisted.

"That's all I took, and I didn't buy anything," the traveler replied.

In recounting the incident later he remarked, "I guess he thought I should travel like the couple I saw in a hotel in Baltimore. They had ten suitcases, and two bellboys were trying to load them on the elevator. I asked the bellboy who was carrying my briefcase if they were going to live there. He informed me they were just going to spend the night. Then he looked at me and asked if that one briefcase was all I had. When I told him it was, he wanted to know how long I was staying. When I told him a week he said, 'A week! Then you have more coming?' I said I didn't know where it would come from. I didn't leave anything behind."

For many years that was the way he traveled: one briefcase with his razor, comb and toothbrush, an extra shirt, a change of underwear, socks, and pajamas. But for the most part the briefcase was jammed with correspondence. He carried his New Testament in his coat pocket. During the last years he traveled, he did add a small zipper airline bag to his brief case. It was small enough to fit under the seat in a plane or go on the luggage rack in a bus which, in the years after his retirement from the General Board of Evangelism, became his principal mode of travel.

"People waste so much time waiting for baggage," he said. "While they are waiting, I am at my destination working. Anyway, the airline will probably lose it, and then you have to do without; so why not do without in the beginning and not worry?"

During the cold weather he did carry an ancient black overcoat that often served as a bed for him in an airport or depot. He never wore a hat and did not carry an umbrella or raincoat. "Why should

I have two coats when my brother has none?" he asked.

Across the years that battered coat became almost a badge, sometimes left behind but never entirely forgotten. During the years he was with the Board, it was left in his office during the summer months. After he retired he either carried it with him or left it at a dry cleaning establishment for the summer where it could be claimed with the advent of cold weather.

In one of his last visits to the headquarters building in Nashville he told of one such happening. He had left his coat the spring before at a cleaning establishment near Lake Junaluska, North Carolina.

This fall I went to get my overcoat because I was starting out and it had begun to get cold. I got it, and after I was back at the Inn I took it out and started looking at it. It wasn't my coat. It was cashmere on the outside. Oh, it was beautiful on the inside as well as the outside. I went back and told the woman there I had the wrong coat.

She said, "No. This is your coat."

I said, "It's not mine. I can't wear anything like that. I have tried it on and it fits perfectly, but it isn't mine."

She said, "A lady came in here not long ago and left this coat for you."

I asked, "What does she look like? What's her name?"

She said, "I don't know. She just told me that she

and her husband love you and want you to have it.
She took your old one and left."

For once his benefactors had outsmarted him.

Once a colleague explained that with the return
of warm weather he would have to get his summer
suits ready for wear. Harry Denman frowned over
his glasses, "Summer suits and winter suits! You mean
you have all that to worry about?"

"Of course. Don't you?"

"No."

"What do you do about getting it cleaned and
pressed?"

"When it needs it and I am in a hotel, I send
it out when I go to bed. It's ready the next morning."

The stories about this traveler with only one suit
are legion, and wherever friends come together there
are countless incidents recounted. Two are verified
by staff members.

As usual, staff members had been telling him for
weeks that he needed a new suit, but he turned a
deaf ear. Then on the opening day of an important
meeting in Miami, where he would be very much
on center stage, the knee of his trousers gave way.
After a hurried consultation, one of the staff men
took him to a nearby men's clothing store. In a matter
of minutes he had selected another dark suit.

"We'll make the alterations and have it ready for
you day after tomorrow," the salesman informed him.

"Day after tomorrow!" Harry Denman exclaimed.
"I'm going to wear it out of here now." And after

a few quick adjustments he did, leaving the old suit behind for the trash basket.

The late J. Manning Potts told of an incident in India. In the heat of Bangalore, Harry Denman realized the one suit needed cleaning and sent it out for a hurry-up job. At the appointed time the suit was not back. Undaunted, Harry Denman, standing six feet tall and weighing well over two hundred pounds, managed to crowd into an extra pair of Dr. Potts's pants, whose owner was five feet six and all of fifty pounds lighter in weight. The hilarity that greeted them in the dining room was such that it quickly traveled back to headquarters where the incident was never forgotten.

Even with a freshly pressed suit, his black tie never seemed to be in the correct place and was usually somewhat the worse for wear. The lock of hair that might have covered the enlarged bald spot usually hung in his eyes, indicating that a haircut was long overdue. Yet he was scrupulously clean. A bath was a daily religious exercise; to him cleanliness was next to godliness. Even in places where bathroom facilities were at a minimum, he would manage at least to have a bucket of water and some soap for his daily bath.

One bishop discovered that to remonstrate him about his appearance had little effect. One morning, after Denman had spent the night sleeping on a bench in a railroad station in Hoboken, the bishop who was to introduce him to a large assembly of women at Buck Hill Falls took one look at his rumpled clothing, his mussed hair, and face little more than half shaved in the depot rest room without benefit of a mirror. He exclaimed, "Harry, you look like the devil. What are those women going to think?"

"They aren't going to think anything, Bishop," he replied. "They are going to be so busy looking at you they won't see me."

However, that was not quite the case. Later in the day when they entered the large assembly room, two women ran up and kissed the rumpled man, completely ignoring the bishop. At that the bishop turned to a friend and remarked, "To worry about Harry is wasted effort. It won't change him, and women adore him just as he is."

In the same fashion he had only one pair of shoes. After there were holes in the soles he would fold up newspaper to keep his feet off the ground until someone noticed his predicament and insisted he go to a shoe store and buy a new pair. The purchase made, he would leave the old pair behind, commenting they had served him long and faithfully, and he hoped the new pair would be as comfortable, but it just took too much time to shop.

To travel light, he seldom carried dictating equipment. He carried a stenographer's notebook and would write his replies in long hand, then rip out the pages and mail them back to his secretary to be typed. Never a good penman under the best of circumstances, he rarely crossed the t's or dotted the i's. His hurried scrawl was made even more illegible by a bouncing airplane or a swaying train or bus. When Lou Dozier, his personal secretary, complained to him about it, he would give her one of his smiles and say, "Lou, you know what I want to say anyway, so say it." And she did.

When he died, he left no extra clothing, no automobile, no stocks or bonds, no real estate. Truly he exemplified Thoreau's adage, "Drive life into a corner and simplify, simplify, simplify." He was a man who gave away everything he had, even his faith, to all with whom he came in contact.

"Things don't bother you until you get them," he often explained.

Many congregations where he preached tried to give him a watch in appreciation for what he had done, but he always managed to refuse. "Why do I need a watch?" he asked. "There are clocks everywhere. Anyway, not having a watch gives me an opportunity to talk with strangers. It is a conversation starter. Besides, when you travel as much as I do you're always changing time. I don't want to bother with that. I just look at the clock when I get there."

He characterized those who carry watches as impatient people. "They keep looking at their watches, wondering when the plane or bus is going to arrive. In church they look at their watches and wonder when the preacher is going to stop talking. You can't concentrate when you're worrying about the time. Besides, it's bad for the health to be so impatient."

For the first few years after he moved to Nashville

from Birmingham, he lived in a hotel. He soon decided a permanent hotel room was unnecessary because he was traveling. Quickly he moved his few treasured photographs to his office. That was about all he had, and he rented a hotel room only for the few nights he was in the city.

When the Board of Evangelism moved to its new building at 1908 Grand Avenue in 1952, a modest apartment in the building was made available for him. It was the nearest thing he had had to a home in fifteen years. On the walls he kept pictures of his mother and Dr. Helen Kim, a few pictures of some close personal friends, and those books which he had not had time to give away.

His office, like his clothing, was in sharp contrast to the offices of many of his colleagues. A wooden table served as a desk. A swivel chair, a straight chair, his prayer kneeling bench, and in later years a big red leather chair comprised the furniture in the carpetless room.

Truly, the things which he valued he valued deeply, and because of the simplicity of his life the things he believed in stood out in sharp relief.

10

HE PRACTICED BROTHERHOOD

Believing so definitely in the fatherhood of God, Harry Denman found the brotherhood of mankind an inescapable fact. For him there was only one true family—the family of God. His letters were punctuated with the phrase, "I pray to our heavenly Father. . . ." He believed the word *our* was all inclusive; it was color blind and racially, economically, socially unbiased. He preached it. He practiced it.

During the time when the question of integration was at the boiling point, he spoke out in his home state of Alabama, "I can speak here but Martin Luther King cannot. Why? Because his skin is dark. Jesus could not speak here. His skin was dark."

Friends believe it was remarks of this nature that cost him election as a delegate to the Jurisdictional and General Conference of The Methodist Church, an honor which had been accorded him four times as a jurisdictional delegate and five times as a delegate to the General Conference.

To his dying day he was to hammer away on the

equality of persons, content to let the chips fall where they might.

On January 19, 1974, in an interview for *The United Methodist Reporter,* he said of his hometown, Birmingham, Alabama, "I was on the board of education of the county. I saw the sins we committed, how we took money from blacks and spent it on white children, how we paid black teachers low salaries. Their buildings were awful; it was almost nauseating. . . . I lived with the Ku Klux Klan. They ran the state—elected our governors and senators. I lived with that. I saw it."

Then he added, "I belong to two churches, one in Birmingham, the other in Nashville, one white and the other black. That's the way to handle integration."

An ever-recurring theme in both his preaching and writing was in answer to the question how a person gets right with God.

I believe the best way to get right with God is to get right with man. I am not sure a person can get right with God unless he first gets right with man. I am not my brother's keeper. I am my brother's brother.

A woman in a church in Kentucky was horrified when I told her I didn't know who a certain TV entertainer was. It was written all over her face. We know all the commentators and all the entertainers in the entertainment world, but we do not know what is in the Book.

Jesus said, "Seek first the Kingdom of God and all these things shall be added unto you." This is the reason we are having so much trouble with integration in the South, and in the nation as far as that is concerned.

Integration is a nationwide problem. Jesus preached the fatherhood of God and the brotherhood of man. We have preached it for thirty or forty years, but we haven't lived it. It is easy to preach, but too hard to live.

Often he spoke out in defense of the Jewish people. He had a lifelong friend who was a Jew. That man is buried in the same cemetery lot in Birmingham with Harry Denman and his mother.

Often Harry Denman said, "I think we must remember Jesus was a Jew, and he was a good Jew. It is strange how much prejudice we can have against Jews, but at the same time say we love Christ. He followed all the Jewish practices and customs, and he knew the law. In fact, he was a son of the law. Jesus was a Jew. We sing, 'O, how I love Jesus,' but do we mean it? Do we love a Jew?"

"The family" at 1908 Grand Avenue, as he often referred to the people at the Board office, was a mixture of races and nationalities.

From the beginning, services in The Upper Room Chapel were integrated with all races being welcome at the Communion table and representatives of all races serving Communion. For more than one person it was a new experience to kneel with a person of a different color or to see black, brown, or yellow hands serving the elements.

While there were signs in the building requesting there be no smoking, there were no signs marking rest rooms, drinking facilities, or the cafeteria according to a color code.

Students from other countries who might need part-time employment found work in the shipping room and offices alongside those who had always resided in the community. Persons from Arabia and Germany might be found wrapping *The Upper Room* to be sent to Australia, while one of Oriental origin might be typing a letter addressed to South America. It was a relationship that all who worked in the headquarters building came to expect.

Always in great demand as a speaker in black churches, Harry Denman said, "I never think of anyone as a person of another race. To me we are just children of God."

Because of his leadership ability, coupled with his tremendous interest in social concerns, there were many demands for his talents as a young man in Birmingham. He became a member of the Kiwanis Club, conference lay leader, president of the Birmingham Council of Religious Education, vice-president of the Alabama Temperance Association, a member of the Jefferson County school board, a trustee of the state training school, and a trustee of Miles College.

From these many positions he was brought into close contact with the problems of the region. He began especially to see the plight of the blacks. Once when the school budget was in jeopardy a labor representative appointed to the board of education suggested the budget be balanced by closing all black schools. For the champion of the unfortunate this was a challenge. Inviting the labor representative to visit the schools with him, he soon had a strong ally in securing a larger apportionment than was then in effect.

About that time he began a drive to register his black friends to enable them to vote, and more than one was afforded this right because of the intervention of the one they came to call their friend. And friend he was.

Speaking to a large assembly of people, he held up a little Testament. "I have people write their names in it," he said. "I heard this man speak. He's from Alabama. I'm from Alabama. We are that much alike anyhow. So after he spoke I asked him to put his name in my Testament and he wrote Martin Luther King, Jr. I liked what he said to the white councils of Alabama. He said, 'Destroy our churches, destroy us, but we are going to love you.' That's spiritual. 'Destroy our church, destroy our families, destroy us, but we are not going to hate you. We are going to love you. We are going to forgive you.' Oh, how I would love to live that way for the spiritual.

"Man looks on the outward appearance, but redemptive love looks on the inside. That's what God looks at."

Writing to Dr. Martin Luther King, Jr. in 1966 he said, "You have a cause for which to live and to die."

In another letter to Dr. King he wrote:

> I lived through the prohibition days. We said that we would always have prohibition, that it was in the Constitution. But we were wrong. We didn't do the educational work that should have been done, and in a few short years the Eighteenth Amendment was repealed.
>
> We have the Civil Rights Bill, but we must see that this law is not only enforced, but that the spirit of the law is lived by all people. I think we need to have a great demonstration of love, and we must come to the place where we recognize a person is a person. It does not make any difference where he is born, or what his color is, or what his economic status is, or his educational attainments.
>
> What we need today is empathy. Some of our Christian leaders have sympathy for racial justice, but what we need is empathy. That is what Jesus had. He always put himself in the place of the other person.

Seldom was a thought so placed in an editorial that it escaped his attention. He was quick to grab the closing sentence in an editorial in *The Christian Advocate* and respond to it in detail:

> I read with great interest your editorial in *The Christian Advocate* for October 17, entitled, "Wallace and The Preachers." You have a great sentence in the closing paragraph of this editorial, "And that culprit

is not the black man, but the white, educated liberal, who has failed to communicate his position to those he would have follow him."

It is a matter of communication, and that communication comes because of deeds of love, not because he is an educated man. His education has given him a trained mind and his liberalism has given him a social passion, but what he needs is deeds of love.

I will tell you a story. A good many years ago I went to a cotton mill town to hold special services. I had been invited by the pastor. He had a lovely home with all the comforts and conveniences, but he did not want to be a pastor in a cotton mill town. I told him I would like to go into the mill and meet the people, but he said he did not care to do so. I went to see the superintendent of the mill and asked him if I could go into the mill and meet the people. He was delighted. He took me to see the overseers and introduced me to each one, and I went through the mill shaking hands with twelve hundred people and asking them to pray for the services in the church.

The trouble is we have built a wall between us and the people. We talk about the wall in Berlin, but we have built a wall. We minister to the owners, and to the superintendents, and to the foremen, but not to the great masses of people. I am speaking about the Methodist Church now because that is the church I know. I have been in it seventy-five years. . . .

We think because we pass resolutions and legislation that does it. We must have legislation, we must have resolutions, but we must have the gospel lived. That is the reason integration is breaking down, because we do not have it in our hearts. . . .

We want color TV, but we do not want color living next door to us. We want the church in the community, but we do not want Christ in the community. I say all of this from the pulpit and people do not like for me to say it; yet I am going to continue to say it.

11

A WORLD MIND

"A few years ago we said the world was a neighborhood. Today we are not a neighborhood. We live in one room. The world has become one room. This being true we must learn to live together. A good way to live together is to pray together. We are one family of many colors, nationalities, and beliefs." So wrote the world traveler in a letter to the International Prayer Fellowship which he was instrumental in founding.

This paradoxical layman, whose life-style can best be summed up as complex simplicity, probably preached to more persons than any other layman and most preachers.

Joining the former prophets of the highways and byways, he became a prophet of the skyways. His hopscotch journeys, spanning mountain ranges and oceans, taking him from continent to continent, were made possible by air travel. His secretary, Lou Dozier, says the miles he traversed can only be stated in terms of millions.

He knew the timetables of the airline far better

than many of the people behind the counter whether in the United States or abroad. He carried an air-travel guide with him, and he consulted it constantly, noting any changes which might be to his advantage. That, plus the fact that he knew so many of the airline personnel and often remembered them with a book or a letter in appreciation for their courtesy, did much to speed him on his way.

"Of course I pray for the captain of the plane," he would say laughingly. "If he gets there, I get there." When he traveled by train he knew the conductors and porters, and they knew him because they soon discovered their joys were his joys, their problems became his problems and a subject for his prayers.

Noting an engagement ring on her finger, he would ask a stewardess about the man she was to marry, and their plans for the wedding, then send them a Bible with his best wishes.

A reporter once described him as an evangelistic gyroscope who spun around the world without a watch in quest of souls.

Not only was he a world traveller, but he was a world citizen, as much at ease with the people of Asia, Africa, or India as in his own office. He ate their food, stayed in their homes, preached in their churches, witnessed to them in their fields and shops, and loved them as his own. Many of them he called his "spiritual children."

Countless students from other countries came to study at American universities and colleges, then returned home to fill important positions because of the encouragement and help of this jet-stream evangelist. Always quick to encourage, he was not averse to using his position as general secretary of one of the major boards in The Methodist Church to open doors for those he felt were deserving. In every way possible he kept informed of scholarships, loans, grants, and outright gifts. He was equally ready to use his own means to shore up one who found the going difficult, and he remained anonymous in the doing.

Never one to be concerned with limitations, he thought in terms of possibilities. If one hundred people came to a meeting he envisioned that next time there would be a thousand. He spearheaded two world convocations on evangelism, one in Philadelphia and one in Washington, D.C., to which world leaders, as well as the rank and file, came by the thousands from the United States and abroad.

During his leadership of the General Board of Evangelism he accepted responsibility for publishing *The Upper Room*, bringing to it two outstanding editors, Roy H. Short, who later became a bishop in The Methodist Church, and J. Manning Potts who shared his enthusiasm for world outreach. With these men and the help of the staff, he saw it become the most widely read daily devotional publication in the world. He saw its circulation climb to one million, two million, three million, and always his cry was more, more, until it was published in thirty-seven languages and Braille.

Church membership could be doubled with a little more effort, he exhorted. Always he preached the need for more churches, more schools, more missionaries, more preachers and lay workers, more hospitals, more food for the starving. His was a spirit that was contagious at home and abroad, and he was ever in the forefront leading the way.

Because he thought big and daring, some of his mistakes, like his accomplishments, were equally big; yet he never was daunted for long. Just because the roof caved in was no reason to be discouraged. Before the pieces could be picked up he had another idea. Harry Denman constantly saw inviting new challenges.

Even while he was traveling behind the Iron Curtain or preaching in Australia, he kept a constant stream of suggestions flowing to his staff, preachers and bishops, politicians, airline officials, hotel managers, and supermarket operators.

"May I suggest . . ." he wrote to an executive, then continued with an outline of his ideas.

From a corporation report he could turn to a housewife at whose table he was eating, and ask, "How much did you pay for these onions?" He would spend an hour rummaging with her through her cupboards, asking about prices, commenting on packaging, and leave with a new fund of knowledge.

Because he could shift gears without stripping them, he could spend an evening with a music student and both of them enjoy it. "Tell me about stereo, Son," he once said, when stereo was first becoming popular. Then he spent the next couple of hours sitting on the floor with the lad while they listened to records. A month or two later there would be a reference to stereo in his sermons, and music lovers in the choir and congregation would smile, feeling sure he understood their world.

He seldom, if ever, watched TV or listened to the radio, and he owned nothing. Nevertheless, he kept abreast of world events meticulously. He was an avid reader. Current events and state, national, and international happenings were his immediate target, as well as any reference to the church, be it Protestant or Catholic. Together with religious periodicals he read *The New York Times, The Wall Street Journal,* and *Time* magazine and quoted from them frequently.

In his office he could scan a weekly circulation report with hundreds of titles and come up with valuable observations that those who worked with it every day had failed to note. If a book showed a great increase in sales he wanted to know the reason why and whether the method used to promote it would help the lagging sales of another.

There was almost no area in the field of human relations with which he was not conversant. If there were one he would find someone he felt knew and proceed to ask probing questions until his own curiosity was satisfied. Often after such a session the one being questioned had the feeling the one doing the questioning had a far greater knowledge of the subject than he had revealed.

Ascetic as a monk, he became even more so when he returned from one of his trips abroad which included India. He thundered out against waste and world hunger. In pulpits across America he shouted, "We are a people surfeited with fat. We stuff even our dogs and fill our garbage cans." With protruding underlip he would hammer the pulpit with his fist and shout, "Look in your garbage cans. Why there's enough in the average one of them to keep a starving child alive for a week, and we throw it away. I've seen little children with bellies swollen from hunger pawing through garbage like little animals searching for food to keep them alive—God's children, starving to death. There's something wrong with a system that allows anything like that to exist in the world while we build bigger barns. If the politicians can't do something about it—our distribution system— maybe we should elect those who can. I've already written to mine. But maybe we ought to do something about it ourselves—stop eating so much, stop wasting so much."

He saw through America's selfish way of dealing with other countries. From pulpits across the nation, when Castro came to power in Cuba, he thundered, "Why weren't we concerned about the poor Cuban people under the dictatorship of Batista? Because he let us run our sugar plantations! Now that Castro has confiscated our gold, we are concerned about the Cubans."

In sharp contrast to this he wrote in one of his meditations for *The Upper Room,* "On the streets of Budapest, Hungary, persons have smiled, greeted me, and pointed to the cross I wear on the lapel of my coat. We could not communicate with our tongues, but we did communicate with our hearts of love."

If there were any one directive in the Bible Harry Denman lived to the last jot and tittle, it was "Go ye into all the world, and preach the gospel to every creature."

Harry Denman was at his absolute best when he had a cause to espouse. Then he could really put on "the rousements."

Usually booked two years in advance, in one year he made four hundred and seven addresses in nineteen countries. "You don't do the work of evangelism behind the desk in a swivel chair," he preached to his staff. True to his belief, he held evangelistic missions on all of the continents and many of the islands. His friends were worldwide.

He went to the people where they lived because he loved them. There was no pretense in his makeup. After preaching and witnessing in a far country he did not go back to a luxurious hotel managed by Americans. In Africa he ate their sadza. In Korea he ate their kimchee and slept on their floors. In India he ate their curry and rice and would have slept out in the open with the homeless had not local pastors insisted that he must not. These outward signs were his visible evidence of identifying with their cause; yet there was an even deeper identification. He always prayed with sincerity and fervor for the country, for the family, and for the individual.

"You go to the people, you love them, you pray with them, and you tell them about God" was the way in which he summed up his travels.

One of his most interesting travelogs is taken from his column "Wander and Wonder." It appeared in *The Methodist Christian Advocate* for January 31, 1961, and later in *Love Abounds*. However, it should be pointed out that for this period his schedule was a bit out of the ordinary.

> Sunday, July 31, I worshiped in Lima, Peru. I was in Lima for the quadrennial meeting of the Central Conference of South America. During the afternoon I went to a worship service for delegates held at the Maria Alvarado School. That night at First Methodist Church, Bishop W. Angie Smith from the United States was in charge of the worship service. Bishop Eleazar Guerra of Mexico translated the English to Spanish and Bishop Sante Uberto Barbieri brought the conference sermon. Also he took an offering for world refugees to be distributed by the World Council of Churches.
>
> The next Sunday, August 7, Dr. J. Manning Potts and I were in Prague, Czechoslovakia. That night we went to the Methodist Church. The pastor, Rev. V. Schneeleerger, brought the message. The sanctuary used to be a dance hall, now we have a sanctuary for worship. Manning Potts and I had attended the executive committee of the World Methodist Council at Zurich, Switzerland.
>
> The next Sunday, August 14, we worshiped with the Methodists in Budapest, Hungary. It was a very won-

derful service. Pastor Adam Hecker brought the message. Both services were high hours of worship.

The next Sunday, August 21, I was at Massanetta Springs, Virginia, for a Bible Conference. I heard Bishop Arthur J. Moore bring the message to a thousand Presbyterians and Methodists from many states in the Union.

The next Sunday, August 28, I worshiped with the laymen of the Rock River Conference at Des Plaines, Illinois. This is where Swedish Methodists had a camp meeting many years. Their descendants have built a beautiful outdoor worship center in memory of those who found spiritual renewal there many years ago. There is a beautiful wooden cross in this lovely setting. I knelt before this cross on Sunday morning and found spiritual renewal in repentance and faith.

The next Sunday, September 1, I was in Seoul, Korea and worshiped at Nam-San Methodist Church with the pastor, my good friend Dr. Hong-kyu-Pyun. The secretary of foreign affairs of the present Korean government is a member of this church and worshiped with us.

The next Sunday, September 11, I worshiped at Frontenac, Wisconsin, with laymen of the St. Paul, Minnesota, District. What a blessed spiritual experience as we sat by the Mississippi River and looked at the cross, as consecrated laymen led us in worship.

The next Sunday, September 18, I worshiped with the Methodists at Sampson County, North Carolina, at Roseboro in a county-wide revival service held in a tabernacle.

The next Sunday, September 25, I worshiped at Williams Town and Mandeville, Manchester Parish, Jamaica, where I was helping in an evangelistic mission under the auspices of the Council of Churches of Jamaica.

What a joy to worship in so many different places! What a privilege to be associated with great Christians in all lands.

12

THEY SHARED A FAITH

HARRY DENMAN and Helen Kim were kindred spirits. Each one had a world personality, and theirs was a dedication that transcended personal desire. They shared a faith that bound them together with the deepest of spiritual ties though for the most part they were separated physically by continents and oceans.

Dr. Kim received her Ph.D. from Columbia University in 1931. She was the first Korean woman to earn a doctorate degree in the United States, and she served as president of Ewha University from 1931 to 1961.

Their courses converged in 1956 when Dr. Helen Kim returned to Seoul from exile in Pusan and began rebuilding Ewha Woman's University. As part of her effort to rebuild the school that had been shattered by the Korean War, she planned a campus revival and invited Dr. Harry Denman to be the evangelist. This was the beginning of a new episode in the life of this lay preacher and witness for Christ. Before Dr. Kim's death in February 1970, Harry Denman

led several evangelistic crusades in Korea with headquarters at Ewha University, the largest woman's
university in the world. Upon a number of occasions
he was instrumental in bringing this woman educator
to the United States where she appeared on the
lecture platform in both national and international
meetings and convocations.

Their correspondence, at first, was highly formal
and businesslike. It was concerned with such matters
as scholarship funds, the executive development
committee for Ewha University, plans for crusades,
the training of lay evangelists, the International
Prayer Fellowship, and salaries for those who would
work with rag pickers, prostitutes, and persons in
prisons in Korea. Soon little messages of tenderness
and mutual concern for one another were included.
They were postmarked from Switzerland, the Philippines, Africa, Europe, India, and many of the islands
of the sea, as well as from the United States and
Korea. While Dr. Kim's letters were personally written in longhand, Dr. Denman's were either dictated
for a secretary to transcribe, or they were more
often written in longhand on notebook paper and
mailed to his office to be typed and remailed to
Dr. Kim.

After a few letters with very businesslike forms
of address and closings, there was soon a change to
"Dear Helen" and "Dear Harry." Dr. Kim concluded
her letters with "Love and prayers." Dr. Denman's
conclusion was "With all good wishes, love and
prayers, I am sincerely your servant."

After a lengthy transoceanic flight, he cabled to his friend in Korea, "Safe. Love. Harry."

On special occasions, birthdays, Christmas, and Easter he would cable, "Prayers and love. Harry."

In December 1962, Harry Denman wrote to Helen Kim, "Well I have just read a most interesting book—the autobiography of Helen Kim. I am in a motel in Kansas. I read it today. What a book! You have lived a life of suffering—yet joy has prevailed in your life. You have been my dear friend for more than six years, yet there are many surprises in this book for me. Some of your activities have never been told. You have walked with kings and have not lost the common touch."

This woman, who had not lost the common touch, could write to Harry Denman from Tokyo and say, "At the arcade store under the Imperial Hotel, I found an interesting store where they had beautiful knives. So I bought one to replace the one you lost in New Delhi. It is of similar size in white silver with five different things in stainless steel attached to it. The five things are knife, scissors, file, can opener, and an awl. Now I will have to wait for you to give me a penny before I can send it to you."

Harry Denman replied, "It was wonderful of you to secure a beautiful knife for me in Tokyo. I appreciate it very much and am enclosing herewith a penny so I can receive this gift from you."

In the spirit of this common touch, Harry Denman wrote to Dr. Kim:

Miss . . . , who is a missionary in Korea, is going to marry a Korean gentleman on March 1st.

I would like to do something for her. I wonder if it is possible according to Korean custom for you to give her a tea and invite missionary friends and Korean friends to come. It would be a tea for the bride. In the United States we have showers and people bring gifts for the bride.

I will take care of the expense of providing the tea and cakes and other things you think are needed. I desire to be the host. I realize I am asking a whole lot, but I would like to do something for this girl. Her mother and father live here in the States. I do not think they will go to the wedding.

Please let me have your frank opinion about the matter.

They moved through fifteen wonderful years of friendship and love, spending only a few snatched hours together.

One time when Dr. Kim was planning a visit to the United States, they tried to arrange a meeting. Dr. Denman wrote, "This letter is written in St. John, Kansas, which is a small town. I will be here through Friday of this week. Then I go to Peoria, Illinois, and then to Grand Island, Nebraska, for four days. Then I have one night engagements in Shreveport, Louisiana, Kansas City, Missouri, and St. Louis, Missouri. Then I come to Dallas to be with you in the planning committee for the International Prayer Fellowship.

"I will be thinking about you on Thanksgiving

Day. I wish I could be with you, but I have these engagements and must keep them."

Regardless of the personal desire they might have felt to be with one another, this was never allowed to interfere with the schedule of commitments. This is so well illustrated by a telegram Helen Kim sent when she had come to New York City for a speaking engagement, "Morning already committed. Come lunch time and talk fast. Love Helen."

While Harry Denman was a prolific letter writer, there were many times when he was weeks, sometimes months behind in his responses even to his dear friend Helen Kim, and so she wrote chiding him.

Dear Harry:
Why don't I hear from you? I made all kinds of allowances and waited for some word all last week. I am sure you must have a good reason.

Upon another occasion when he had fallen behind in his correspondence with her, this man who was used to working out of difficult situations, wiggled off the hook with complete calm. "I left Birmingham on October 28 and went to eight states in evangelistic missions. I was preaching, teaching, praying, visiting, and counseling. I returned to Birmingham December 16. The Lord took good care of me. My mail suffered, and now I am trying to take care of it."

However, there were times when he kept the postman busy. Helen Kim once wrote, "I have several letters from you to answer at once. They are dated

January 22, January 24, January 31, and February 4. They were hand-written by you from Taipei."

Of all the countries in which he traveled and preached, perhaps Harry Denman felt a closer kinship to Korea than any other place on the globe. He especially loved to hear the Korean people sing. He cried with them, prayed with them, ate with them, witnessed to them, and loved them into the kingdom of God.

It was through this understanding relationship of the educator and the evangelist that hundreds upon hundreds of persons, especially the girls of Ewha University, were led to Christ. In 1961 when Dr. Denman was there in a crusade, 1,289 persons were baptized in one service. Fourteen preachers and two bishops participated in the service.

Dr. Kim told about the events:

As part of our seventieth anniversary program we scheduled one week in November as Spiritual Emphasis Week. From the beginning years, ever since I can remember, our institution always had a week of revival meetings each year. But under the Japanese occupation and in the confusion of liberation and war, we had been unable to continue this particular event. All of us were being deprived by our own negligence of the special opportunity to grow in Christian grace from year to year. The seventieth anniversary was a good year to restore this program for our rehabilitation as persons with souls, along with the rehabilitation of our buildings and equipment.

To lead our meeting we found a man of God and a lover of Korea and its people in the person of Dr. Harry Denman, the general secretary of the Board of Evangelism of The Methodist Church in the United States. His simple and direct messages won many hearts to Christ and stimulated lukewarm Christians to return to a glowing faith. Hundreds of our students and faculty were led to embrace the Christian faith for the first time or to recommit themselves to Christ and rededicate themselves to follow him in the service of man.

The second year, Dr. J. Manning Potts, editor of *The Upper Room*, came. Dr. Denman and Dr. Potts returned year after year with teams of outstanding pastors, laymen, and laywomen. . . .

Literally thousands of our young men and women and girls and boys have come into contact with the person of Christ. They have been challenged to his way of life and have committed themselves to his cause. We have seen some of these wonders and miracles performed on our campus as well as on other campuses throughout Korea.

Friends tell of often seeing them after a great revival service walking together across the campus of Ewha University. Dr. Kim, diminutive and immaculate in her flowing Korean gown, rested her tiny hand on the arm of the disheveled and rumpled man from the United States who towered above her. He peered down at her over the rim of his glasses, smiling, talking softly, or just walking quietly. They strengthened one another with their shared faith in the loving God whom they served.

13

SINCERELY YOUR FRIEND

Staff members recall a particularly trying day of meetings when Harry Denman joined a group in prayer. At the conclusion of his prayer, instead of the traditional Amen, he said, "Sincerely your friend, Harry Denman." That is the way he signed his letters. It was the way in which he thought. He was a friend to hundreds of thousands of people around the world.

For those who knew the man, not only was this in character, but it was in keeping with his total philosophy of life. He loved the Lord with all of his heart, but he also loved his neighbor more than himself. Perhaps nowhere is this spirit better seen than in his letters which for years kept a battery of secretaries busy.

And he wrote to all—politicians, corporation executives, educators, bishops, porters, convicts, persons in hospital beds. His suggestions, his words of encouragement, and his warm-hearted friendship were available to all.

He was always deeply appreciative of courtesies extended to him and wrote many notes of thanks.

Mothers and grandmothers were very special to this man without a family. As he traveled he became acquainted with many, and as a result he learned about their families. To one who had been especially helpful in the claims department of an airline he wrote after reading an article about her son, "Congratulations on the wonderful service your son is rendering in the field of medicine and healing."

As quick to complain as commend, he wrote to the vice-president in charge of customer relations for a large airline:

> When I boarded your plane the counter agent said I would have a snack breakfast, which is all that is necessary.
>
> I do not drink coffee. That is strange, but I do not.
>
> The stewardess said I could have hot tea and I agreed. After a while she came back and said she was sorry but they did not have any tea. I decided to take milk. Again she came and said they did not have any milk.
>
> There is nothing you can do about it now, but I want you to know about it. I do not see any use of serving a snack on this flight. Why not abolish it?

As always, the closing was, "Sincerely your friend."

Because of the countless miles he traveled, he was known and loved by airline employees the world over. He prayed with them, discussed their plans for marriage, sent them books, and often would write to parents telling them what an outstanding job their daughters were doing as stewardesses.

The high regard which the crews had for him was demonstrated when he returned to Nashville after his first preaching mission around the world. Several staff members and their families went out to the airport to greet him.

One by one the passengers came down the steps from the big plane. Finally a disheveled man, carrying a briefcase, emerged and stood for a moment blinking into the lights before he began a slow descent. Friends started forward, but two airline stewardesses, smart in their uniforms, raced out from the terminal to meet him at the foot of the stairs. Throwing their arms around him, they shouted, "Where have you been?" and kissed him. Smiling broadly, the rumpled man with two beautiful girls, one on either arm, marched triumphantly into the terminal.

Perhaps a letter written to the president of one of the major airlines indicates the reason for the affection these girls felt for him. To the president he wrote:

> Recently I flew on one of your planes. There were ninety-three persons aboard, twenty-four first class and sixty-nine tourists. We had three stewardesses. They did a magnificent job. We were flying one hundred fifty minutes. They sold cocktails, served meals and sold beers.
>
> One young lady had a radiant smile. She walked down that aisle many times with full trays. She had enthusiasm and vitality. Finally the smile disappeared. The elasticity of her step slackened. She was tired.

The three young women were on their feet one hundred fifty minutes.

I hope you can put another stewardess on a flight that is full of passengers.

A popular magazine had an article, "Too Tired to Love." I do not want the stewardesses on your airline "Too tired to be radiant."

Two sentences in a letter from Senator John Sparkman from Alabama sum up so well the friendship and admiration these two men had for one another. "Harry, it is always refreshing to have a note from you. You are a wonderful man for whom all who know you are grateful."

He wrote to the editor of the *Wall Street Journal,* who was about to retire, "Who is going to give us these heart-searching messages when you are no longer editor?

"I am glad we are to be inspired and informed by your column from time to time.

"Also I hope you will be contributing editor for the *New York Times* on its expanded editorial page. I wish you could have a column in the *Times* called 'Words to be Lived.' Four letter words to be lived. Hope—love—life—good—save—give—just —time—seek—best—come—deed—duty—hear —need—tame—work. There is no Christianity unless it is lived.

"These four letter words must become flesh."

In the same outgoing mail in which he wrote the publisher of a large newspaper protesting vigorously the increase in subscription price, he also responded to an inquiry, "What is the Good News?"

"The Good News is that God forgives when we have an obedient faith in him and sacrificial love for all persons."

Upon learning that the wife of a friend had died, he wrote, "I am certainly sorry to hear about the death of the body of your wife. She is not dead, only her body is dead. She is living with her living Christ in the Eternal City. The flesh fades and dies, but the spirit quickens and lives forever. We thank God for our belief in the everlasting life."

Quick to identify rather than point the finger, he advised one who had asked for help, "All of us live either in the garden of disobedience or the garden of obedience. If we live in the garden of disobedience we are bringing death and sin into the world. If we live in the garden of obedience we are bringing life and salvation into the world.

"The First Adam disobeyed God in the garden and brought sin and death into the world. The second Adam obeyed God in the garden and brought salvation and life into the world."

Letters of inquiry came to him from all over the world, and from many persons he had never met. One such letter, written in pencil on copy book paper, stated, "You and I have never met, but last night in our prayer group I heard your message via tape. I am asking you to pray for me and for our church that we will be open enough to receive the Holy Spirit without reservations or restrictions."

To that request he replied, "We cannot put restrictions on the ministry of the Holy Spirit. We either obey or we do not.

"The temptation is to have our way instead of God's way. Jesus loved all persons except one—himself. I went through the four Gospels and could not find that Jesus ever committed a selfish act."

Always the champion of young people, when questioned about the Jesus People, he replied:

> I think they are great. They love Jesus. They love all persons. What I am trying to do is to get the senior citizens to be Jesus People.
>
> The young people are unafraid and undefeated. They have dynamic courage and holy boldness.
>
> The old people are full of fear instead of faith, full of indifference instead of love, full of defeat instead of victory, full of materialism instead of the spiritual, and full of self instead of God.
>
> The teenager asks today, "Why don't you live outside the walls of the church what you say inside the walls of the church?"

When a mother was having trouble with her children, he replied, "You say you love them. Of course you love them. You say you give them everything you have. What they want is affection. We think when we give our young people material things they will understand we love them, but they don't understand it. We think they realize we love them, but somehow they do not get the idea."

His flood of mail did not slacken with his retirement. It became more personal, and he had more time to reply though his secretarial help was limited. In writing to the author of an editorial, he showed his continued interest in his country and the world.

> Thank you for your editorial. It is a challenge to all of us.
>
> The greatest need we have in the United States today is to have a prophet whose text will be "In God We Trust" and who will tell us about our national and individual sins which are destroying us.
>
> God bless you.

And, as always, he closed this letter

> Sincerely your friend,
> Harry Denman

14

THE QUESTION AND ANSWER MAN

Harry Denman had some very definite theological opinions, and he took the Holy Bible for his authority. Perhaps the best insight into his theology is to be seen in the unique way in which he responded to questions that came to him. He never side-stepped the issue. He seldom debated the issue, yet he made his position clear to clergy and laity alike.

Q. What is your belief concerning the second coming of Christ?

A. If you will read the twenty-fourth chapter in the Gospel of Matthew in the New English Bible there are some points to consider.

While it is true that a good many people expected his immediate return to establish his kingdom, he is not coming back until the heavenly Father says for him to come. That may be any time or it may be a long way off. I do not think we can know when his coming is near. He says in this chapter there are going to be false Messiahs, so I am not going to put my wisdom up against God's wisdom.

Folks ask if I am anxious to see him coming in

the clouds of heaven. I tell them I do not have any great desire to see him coming or not to see him coming. I am trying to do my best to be ready when he comes and get people to be ready.

I think my loving heavenly Father has more wisdom than I have. When he wants Jesus to return, Jesus will return. It does not make any difference what I think about it. Even if I am anxious for him to come, or if I pray for his return, I do not believe it will change God's plans in this regard.

I think people should know he is coming. I believe he is coming for I believe what the Bible says. . . .

We may want Christ to come, and I presume all of us do, but we do not have to wait for his physical appearance because we can have his Spirit living in us.

As you know, Paul said, "For me to live is Christ." He also said, "Christ liveth in me."

I go into many homes and find this plaque on the wall, "I am going to be with Jesus someday." I think it means, of course, they believe they will be with Jesus when their body dies. But they do not have to wait for their body to die in order to be with Jesus. They can have him now.

Personally I am glad our Lord is giving us more time to work and tell the unsaved about the Savior. He is giving us more time to tell people who are indifferent about the love of Christ for them. I think the important thing for Christians to do is to witness to the love of our blessed Lord. I think also when we tell them about his love we should tell them he is going to return and we hope they are ready for him when he comes.

Q. Should we have only one church?

A. I think we must work with other Christians if we are going to win the world for Christ and establish his Kingdom. I do not believe in organic union, but I do believe in Christian unity. We do have the National Council of Churches in order that we can work together. If we did not have these organizations we would be organizing one because Christians have to work together.

The laboring people find there is great strength in their unions and labor federations. The manufacturers have their organizations. I think Christians ought to be united in movements that will help them work together. I do not believe in having one church because I do not think that is what God intended. I think we are different people. We have different churches, but we ought to have an ecumenical movement which will help us to work together in this business of fighting evil and darkness.

Q. Do you believe in miracles?

A. When I was in Tulsa, Oklahoma, I went to see Dr. Oral Roberts at his great university. In his office there were three words on his desk in the form of a motto, "Expect a Miracle."

I preached on that not long ago. I do not think we are expecting miracles. This is what happened in the days of Jesus as recorded in the New Testament. When people believed in him miracles happened. When they did not, nothing happened.

I think we ought to expect miracles, and I am indebted to Oral Roberts for receiving this inspiration.

Q. How could Jesus say, "Blessed are the meek," and then get angry?

A. Jesus did say, "Blessed are the meek for they shall inherit the earth." But I think if you read the third chapter of Mark's Gospel in the King James Version you will find that Jesus became angry because of the hardheartedness of the religious people.

Q. Was Jesus a Christian?

A. I think we must define our terms.

For example, Mr. John Wesley was never a Methodist, and yet he is the founder of the Methodist Church. Mr. Wesley had a great spiritual experience at Aldersgate. He realized his sins were forgiven. He realized he did trust Christ and Christ only for salvation.

He was a priest in the Church of England and wanted the church to have this experience. He remained an Anglican priest as long as he lived, but he was the founder of the Methodist Church.

Jesus had a great experience in the wilderness when he determined that God was going to be first in his life. He was going to live by the word of God and by the will of God and worship God and him only. . . . I think Jesus was a good Jew. He certainly was a God-centered man. And people came to him because they saw God in him.

We are Christian because we live as Christ lived and people see Christ living in us.

We do not live according to the law, but we live according to grace. We are saved by grace. It is the grace of God. And we are saved because of our faith in Christ.

Q. What is the greatest test of our Christianity?

A. Our behavior. You can tell what a person believes by the way he or she behaves.

Q. Isn't it impossible to love some people?

A. I am not sure we can love one another unless we put our faith in Christ and are trusting him for salvation. After we do this, we can love one another because Christ said, "Love one another as I have loved you."

Q. What about those who refuse to accept the love of God?

A. If people will not accept the love of God, then of course, they know nothing about his love. They never have the experience of his forgiving love and his redemptive love and his healing love and his eternal love and his witnessing love. . . .

If a person does not want salvation, then God is not going to force it. That is one of the reasons why I love God, because he gives me the right of choice. I can accept his forgiving love, his redeeming love, or I can reject it, but he still loves me. He does not turn against me because I do not accept his love, but if I refuse then the fault is mine not his.

Q. How do we discover the will of God for us?

A. Take Today's English Version of the Bible which is the Good News for Modern Man and read Romans chapters 12 through 15. Paul tells us exactly how to know whether or not it is the will of God.

Q. Are we wrong in not observing the seventh day as the Sabbath?

A. If I were you I would not be greatly concerned about the seventh day of the week and the first day of the week. The Old Testament teaches that the seventh day of the week was for rest. We believe the first day of the week is the day of the Resurrection. God has made this a holy day by raising Jesus from the dead.

In my own thinking, I try to think that every day is a holy day and I shall live every day in the same way.

Q. What is the proper form of baptism?

A. I am not going to debate the form or method.

I was baptized in the name of Jesus Christ. I was not immersed, but I was baptized by a minister who will baptize anyone regardless of color who puts their faith in the Lord Jesus Christ. Water does not save anyone. It is faith in Jesus Christ that saves. Water baptism is a confession that we have repented of our sins and we are putting our trust in Christ.

I think the Methodist Church has the right idea. We baptize people the way in which they desire, either by sprinkling, by pouring, or by immersion.

I think any person who believes would like to be baptized. However, the Quakers do not have any baptism of water. For them it is the baptism of the spirit, and Quakers are very fine Christian people. In fact, I have found that some of them are quite unusual Christians.

Q. Do you believe in praying for guidance?

A. I ask so many people what they pray for, and they tell me they pray for God's guidance. Certainly I believe in prayer, but I also think God is more than anxious to guide us. He loves us and wants to guide us in the best possible way of life. I think what we ought to pray is that we will accept his guidance for our lives.

I ask people this question, "Do you believe God's will for your life is perfect?" Usually they answer, "Yes." Then I say, "Why are you always trying to change it? Why not accept his will for your life?" The answer, of course, is we like to have our own way.

Self destroys self. We want to be God. Sometimes we want to be greater than God. Consequently we are destroying ourselves.

Q. Should church property be taxed?

A. The business property of the church should be taxed. What we use for the worship of God and for Christian nurture and for the living quarters of the ministers should not be taxed.

Q. Can we learn anything from the Eastern religions?

A. I think our Western Christianity ought to take some of the habits of the Eastern religions, and one is the spirit of meditation. The Hindus spend much time in meditation. I think that as followers of our Lord Jesus Christ we ought to meditate and listen to him.

The Bible says Jesus went to a lonely place for

prayer. I am sure he went to listen to his heavenly Father and then he obeyed him. I do not think it helps to listen if we are not going to obey.

Q. I find it so difficult to forgive. Does this mean that I am not a Christian?

A. All Christians should be in the forgiving business. I forgive because Jesus said, "If you have a grievance against anyone, forgive him so that your Father in heaven may forgive you the wrongs you have done."

I believe it is necessary for me to have the forgiving love of Christ in my heart and life if I am to have forgiveness. I think every Christian should be full of forgiving love because if we are not then we can never receive God's forgiving love. And we pray of course what we call the disciples' prayer, "Father, forgive us as we have forgiven."

15

WITNESS AND LIVE

ONE MAN SAID, "You really want to know what Harry Denman meant in my life? In military terms he meant *about-face*, a complete one-hundred-eighty-degree turn. My business was gone and my wife was about to leave me. When I heard him, I was depending on liquid courage. That's expensive, and it doesn't solve any problems.

"Dr. Denman came to speak at a men's retreat about one hundred miles from where we were living at that time. Two of my friends wanted me to go. At first I made excuses. Actually I didn't have the money. But they said they would pay my way, and my wife urged me to go. So I went.

"Today I suppose we would say that he told it like it was. At least it came through to me, for when I compared myself to him the picture wasn't pretty. When you're down and desperate you either go up or out. I wasn't ready to go out, so I went up. It was mighty tough at first, but I made it, all the way.

"Today our home is an affirmation of the saying that the family that prays together stays together.

It's been a good many years since I went to that retreat, but I have never forgotten.

"Harry knew long before he died what he meant to us. He stayed in our home upon occasion. He was a great soul."

Probably in every community where Harry Denman preached and witnessed, there were changed lives. Today a very prominent churchman says, "I can remember so well when Dr. Denman came to hold a revival in our church. One evening we were having several of our senior high group in after the services. We invited him to come with us, and somewhat to our surprise he came.

"We thought he was good in the pulpit, but honestly he was at his best sitting on the floor with us, talking with us, telling us stories. Somehow the conversation just seemed to go in the direction he wanted it to go. Suddenly, rather than talking about football and parties, we were talking about Jesus Christ. He did it so naturally, so easily, we were not embarrassed to talk about something we had always been hesitant to talk about before. It has made it easier for me ever since."

Truly Harry Denman had a way with young people and children. His files are filled with letters and pictures—pictures of graduations, weddings, families, drawings made by little children, notes of love; and he responded in kind. After he was a guest in a home, he often wrote to the children before he wrote to the parents. "Children like to get mail," he would explain; and so he wrote to them, and they to him. It was a correspondence that often continued from early grade school even to retirement.

One father wrote, "You have meant so much to our family. You have opened so many gates and doors. Our lives would have been quite different but for you. You have been the best friend we ever had. We love you for the influence for good you have been in the life of our family."

Responding to a girl with whom he had been corresponding for many years, and who was about to marry a boy of the Jewish faith, he wrote, "I am thankful that you are a very wise woman and that you are not going to try to change the religion of J. . . . He has a wonderful religion. He has the same religion which Jesus had. I am sure he is trying to live according to the teachings of his religion.

"My friend, Sigmund Bauer, was such a good friend I thought I ought to give him the invitation to become a Christian. He came to our church services and to all of our activities. Of course he went to the Temple almost every Friday night. One day I talked to him about it and asked if he would become a Christian. He said, 'No. I'll stick to my religion.'

"He knew the New Testament and was always showing us how we fail to keep the teachings of Christ. I think that is the reason a good many Jews do not become Christians, they know we do not live the New Testament.

"I think God's love ought to be seen in our lives. And I have seen some Jews who seem to have more of the love of God than some Christians. So I want you to live the best possible life as a Christian. I think your love of God ought to be greater than his love of God."

Harry Denman, a bachelor, showed love and concern for girls and women. They adored him in return. The picture of a beautiful high school girl was the bookmark in one of his Bibles.

Just how this great outpouring of love was given and received is indicated in a letter which Harry Denman kept from a woman whose love he treasured for many, many years, and who with her husband returned that love.

She wrote, "I'm ashamed I don't write to you more often and tell you how much I love you and what you have meant in our lives. When I began to write this letter I was floored with the impossibility of ever trying to find enough words to adequately thank you for everything you have done for us, because your expressions of love have been legion.

"I began to reminisce on the first thrill you ever gave me—the first time I realized I meant something special to you. In my mind's eye I saw again a big box of chocolate candy you sent me at Winnataska for my first summer camp. I was so thrilled. I felt so important. I don't think any of the other girls got packages from anybody except family.

"It was you who sent me my first flowers, and all the flowers I ever received except from John. You sent them on every important occasion. I remember red carnations at Christmas in 1923; sweet peas on the occasion of my first piano recital, red roses at the close of the annual oratorical contest, red roses on my graduation, and a corsage of pink rose buds to go with my pink dress when I did "An Evening Story."

"I remember your going with me to college. We sat together on one of those long side benches on the street car. I sat close to you and loved you for going with me. Indeed, I knew I wouldn't be going at all if it had not been for you. I knew you arranged the scholarship that paid for my tuition. It was you who arranged for me to grade freshmen English papers to help pay my way. It was you who helped me get my first teaching job.

"Again it was you who came to my aid when I needed you so desperately. John was ill. . . . We borrowed all we could, but I needed a job to pay his sanatorium bill. I didn't have any business education. All I knew was how to teach school. They wouldn't let married women teach, but you pleaded my cause so eloquently they made an exception in my case. I don't know what I would have done without you. John and I will never forget, nor cease being grateful to you.

"We'll always love you for coming to us at Mama's death. John was responsible for letting you know. You had already left Birmingham and were in Nashville. It was John who said, 'I am going to call Mr. Harry.' He always did, and still does, call you 'Mr. Harry.' It was just like Mr. Harry to come. You were always near when I needed you.

"You will never, never know what you have meant to me through the years nor what a great influence you have been on my life. Anything good I may have done or thought has been engendered and sparked by you.

"When I feel warm inside and yearn for a better me it is because I think of you, your faith in me, and all you have done for me.

"There is no way in the world I can repay you for all you have done for me except to pass it on to another, and that is what John and I have tried to do. He loves you as much as I for opening so many doors of opportunity for us."

In one of the letters received after Harry Denman's death, a minister wrote, "I first met him when I was a boy of twelve. Because of that, and subsequent meetings when I was with him, there was a profound change in my life not only because of what he said, but because of his example.

"Many, many times I have quoted Harry Denman right along with St. Paul. There are so many similarities."

A businessman from North Dakota perhaps expressed the feeling of both youth and adults when he wrote, "When I hear the name of Harry Denman I have a wonderfully warm feeling. Harry was not only my friend, he was my inspiration. I had the privilege of listening to him and visiting with him only eight or nine times, but each time I came away a better man and Christian.

"The first time I saw and heard Dr. Denman was

at a Methodist conference. I thought I was a Christian, but when he said, 'Whoever denies me before men, I also will deny before my Father who is in heaven,' something lifted me right out of the pew and carried me down to the altar where I publicly confessed Jesus as my Lord and Savior. Things had been happening in my life the months just before this, but that was the climax, the giving of myself to Christ.

"The last time we were with Harry was at an Ashram in Montana. The only reason we went, or so we reasoned then, was to be with him and worship our Lord together. He was then, and still is, an inspiration to me, and I thank God for this humble servant.

"My wife and I have just finished rereading his little tract, 'Witness and Live.' That was, and is, Harry Denman."

After some years of retirement, Harry Denman gave a brief meditation based on the scripture "Love will never come to an end." He illustrated it with a personal experience:

It was nine o'clock on Father's Day morning. The telephone rang in my room at the Decatur Inn in Decatur, Alabama. I thought, "Who is calling me? No one knows where I am." I was supposed to be in another motel, but my host pastor had changed my reservation.

It was Barbara, my daughter in the Spirit. She is the wife of a pastor. Her father was a pastor. She has two lovely daughters.

She gave me a message of love for Father's Day. She said, "Last year on Father's Day you were sick and in the hospital. We could not call you, but now you are preaching again, and we send our love and thank God for answered prayer."

My daughter in the Spirit remembered. It takes no effort to forget, but it does take energy to remember. Love remembers."

This man who had no family treasured his spiritual families, and his files are filled with notes of love which he kept tucked away from the eyes of the world. A letter from a woman written on light blue stationery and in a beautiful script has this paragraph, "Today I am remembering many things about you, a meal you shared with us, an anecdote you told, the little devotional books you sent the boys, the beautiful olive wood Bible you sent me at my high school graduation. I don't even know your address since you retired, but I trust you will get this letter."

16

RETIREMENT

W HEN THE calendar indicated that Harry Denman was nearing the mandatory retirement age of seventy-two, he was not around for farewell dinners or to help in the selection of his successor. He was halfway around the world engaged in a preaching mission in India. His retirement began April, 1965. However, he left Nashville the last day of December, 1964, and did not return to the headquarters building until long after a new general secretary had been elected.

Prior to his retirement, members of the Board and staff had urged him to accept living quarters and office space in Nashville. He refused and elected to continue his nomadic life-style. He wrote to a friend, "My mailing address is still Nashville, but I never go there. I do not have a home. I do not have any relatives. I do not have an office. I go from place to place, from city to city, from motel to motel, from person to person, witnessing for our Lord, Jesus Christ."

More than a year later he wrote to another friend,

"I enjoy riding a bus, and I can sleep on a bus because we have those wonderful highways with buses that roll along at seventy-five miles per hour."

To another he said, "Now I see the places I used to fly over. It is good to see the towns and countryside. It is an education to ride a bus. There are all types of people there."

Across the years he had developed the art of avoiding the customary farewells at the end of a preaching engagement. A previously alerted layman would slip him away while the pastor pronounced the benediction. After retirement he continued this practice but now it was usually to a bus station rather than to an airport. He often rode the bus all night and far into the following day. In that way he could avoid the expense of a night in a hotel or motel.

During the many years he served the General Board of Evangelism, he never drew his full salary with the exception of his last year, and that he gave to the Foundation for Evangelism. For the most part he took only enough money to pay the premiums on several health insurance policies and for his meager personal wants. As general secretary his living quarters were provided for him while he was in Nashville, and he had an expense account while traveling. After retirement, he very often felt financial pressure because his traveling expenses were high. Many of the honorariums he received from his speaking engagements would not cover the costs. Still he continued to travel, to preach, and to witness.

In August, 1967, a blood clot developed on his

brain, and he underwent surgery for its removal. He was not incapacitated for too long, and he was soon back on the road. As other complications developed in 1974, he was in and out of the hospital for the better part of a year. Yet he continued to force himself.

In addition to his preaching, he was instrumental in forming an American chapter of the International Prayer Fellowship, an organization that had begun in Korea. At Lake Junaluska Assembly in North Carolina, which became the office for the Prayer Fellowship, a prayer room was named for him.

Because of failing health, friends and doctors prevailed upon him to enter Fair Haven Retirement Home in Birmingham in March, 1975. Whenever his strength would permit, he continued to preach. He preached three times on Sunday, July 4, 1976, on a two-point charge in northern Alabama. He preached in each of the two churches on Sunday morning and to both congregations who had come together that evening in one of the churches. For this he was paid with a load of watermelons which he took back to Fair Haven Retirement Home for the residents.

In September, 1976, he held his last preaching mission, speaking twelve times in a week at Tuscumbia, Alabama. Completely exhausted, he entered a hospital in Birmingham shortly thereafter.

While he could no longer preach he could still pray and write letters. To some friends he wrote, "I desire to have the obedient faith in God that Jesus had. I desire to love all persons as sacrificially as Jesus did."

Then at the bottom of his letter he drew a cross, saying "This is the church." The horizontal beam was labeled, "Sacrificial love for all persons." The vertical beam carried the words, "Obedient faith in God."

17

EPILOGUE

Harry Denman never slowed down. Finally his body was unable to comply with the demands he placed upon it. Days and nights of travel, strange beds when he paused to find a bed, meals at all hours and sometimes no meals, a grueling speaking schedule, and tremendous responsibility finally exacted their toll.

A longtime friend, J. Tal Murphree, writing in Evangelade Echoes, gives a poignant description of Harry Denman in the closing months of his life.

"That incomparable Harry Denman! When I arose to speak in Birmingham, there he sat on the front pew.

"When I finished my sermon and the closing hymn had been sung, the pastor asked Harry Denman to express the benedictory prayer. On the next few moments converged the elements of his personality in a cross-blending that will be unforgettable to those who were present. With the image of a patriarch and the dignity of a general, he stepped to the front and faced the congregation. His voice was deep and rich, and powerful with pathos. 'Jesus, help us to love people,' he prayed. 'You did! Help us to love the thief, the immoral, the unlovely. You did!' By this time his strong voice had risen almost to a shout. Then with the disarming sincerity he added, 'Help me to love all those cranky folks at Fair Haven.'

"And the congregation, moved to tears, almost cracked up."